rooms
your kids
will love

rooms
your kids
will love

50 fun & fabulous decorating ideas and projects

PAIGE
GILCHRIST

LARK
BOOKS

A Division of
Sterling Publishing Co., Inc.
New York, NY

PAIGE GILCHRIST
editor

CHRIS BRYANT
art director

EVAN BRACKEN
photographer

BARBARA ZARETSKY
cover designer

ORRIN LUNDGREN
illustrator

VERONIKA ALICE GUNTER
HEATHER SMITH
assistant editors

RAIN NEWCOMB
editorial assistant

HANNES CHAREN
production assistant

SPECIAL PHOTOGRAPHY

VNU Syndication

Alexander van Berge

Dennis Brandsma

Paul Grootes

Dolf Straatemeier

George v.d. Wijngaard

Hans Zeegers

Library of Congress Cataloging-in-Publication Data

Gilchrist, Paige.
    Rooms your kids will love : 50 fun & fabulous decorating ideas
and projects / by Paige Gilchrist.
      p.   cm.
    Includes index.
    ISBN 1-57990-429-7
    1. Handicraft.   2. Children's rooms.   3. Interior decoration.   I. Title.

TT157.G457 2002
747.7'7—dc21   2001038398

10 9 8 7 6 5 4 3 2 1

Published by Lark Books, a division of Sterling Publishing Co., Inc.,
387 Park Avenue South, New York, N.Y. 10016

First Paperback Edition 2003
© 2002, Lark Books

Distributed in Canada by Sterling Publishing, c/o Canadian Manda Group,
One Atlantic Ave., Suite 105, Toronto, Ontario, Canada M6K 3E7

Distributed in the U.K. by: Guild of Master Craftsman Publications Ltd.
Castle Place, 166 High Street, Lewes, East Sussex, England, BN7 1XU
Tel: (+ 44) 1273 477374 • Fax: (+ 44) 1273 478606
Email: pubs@thegmcgroup.com • Web: www.gmcpublications.com

Distributed in Australia by Capricorn Link (Australia) Pty Ltd.,
P. O. Box 704, Windsor, NSW 2756, Australia

If you have questions or comments about this book, please contact:
Lark Books
67 Broadway
Asheville, NC 28801
(828) 253-0467

Printed in China

ISBN 1-57990-429-7

contents

FIRST STEPS 10

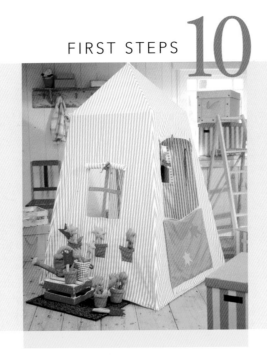

WILD KINGDOMS 16

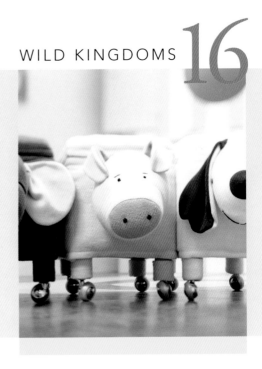

9
INTRODUCTION

THE SUN,
MOON & STARS 30

SECRET
GARDENS 40

OCEAN VIEW 60

COLOR THEIR WORLD 72

STOW IT AWAY 92

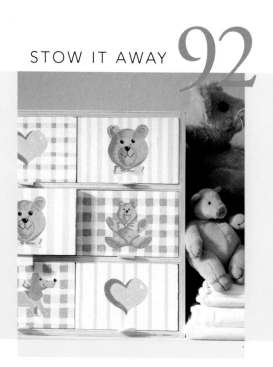

BASIC TECHNIQUES 110

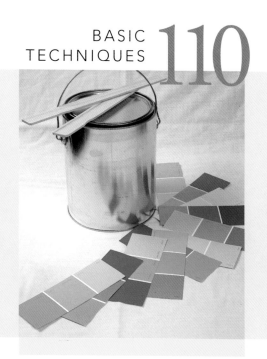

120 PATTERNS

126 ACKNOWLEDGMENTS
CONTRIBUTORS

127 INDEX

INTRODUCTION

EVEN IF YOU LEAVE ALL FOUR WALLS COMPLETELY BARE, dress the windows with nothing but plain white shades, and equip the space with little more than something to sleep on, marvelous things will happen in your child's room. This is the place where he or she will give up bottles, practice toddling across the floor, learn to tie shoes, and (it will seem to you) grow inches overnight. With or without curtains that match the comforter, regardless of whether there are storybook characters frolicking across the walls, your child's room will be a bustling little center of creativity, camaraderie, inquiry, and all kinds of self-expression—you can count on it.

That's why the first step in thinking about decorating your little one's room is to relax. You're not going to stunt anyone's growth and development by choosing the wrong paint color or failing to add enough flourishes. Remember, what you're really doing is providing a backdrop for a lot of spontaneously combusting coming of age; it's awfully hard to go wrong. The second step is to join in the fun. There'll be plenty of that happening naturally. All you have to do is encourage it, echo it, and add to it (the nurture half of the equation, you might say). We've created a book loaded with doable ideas for how.

We've come up with 50 fabulous projects to make to dress up your child's room. And we've organized them around motifs kids are naturally drawn to: animals, flowers, bright colors, and so on. The idea isn't to give you recipes for elaborate theme rooms that no busy parent has the time to pull off. Rather, it's to show you how easily basic techniques can be adapted to create whatever sort of atmosphere you're after. We've also kept in mind a basic truth about children: they grow. And change—change their preferences, change their list of favorites, change their minds. The last thing you want to do is overhaul an entire room the minute red trains are out and purple wizards are in. We give you ideas that are easy to modify over time, and we demonstrate how

adding simple touches (a painted chair or a decorated lamp, for example) is often the best way to define a room's character. Finally, knowing it's difficult to think about decor if you can't see past the clutter kids naturally generate, we devote a hefty chapter to the subject of storage.

The book's dozens of projects make inventive use of standard craft techniques and do-it-yourself decorating approaches. If you're happiest wielding a paintbrush, we'll show you how to cover a wall with polka dots and stripes, give a hardwood floor a painted-in-place "rug," and decorate a plain chest of drawers with a bright plaid pattern. Prefer simple woodworking? You can make rolling toy carts, handy ledges for displaying sports trophies and storing dolls, and simple scroll-saw animals to dress up furniture and walls. If you're on friendly terms with a sewing machine, there are projects for whipping up every thing from playful throw pillows to an embroidered mobile. And if you see yourself as more of a generalist, you'll find clever ideas for embellishing mirror frames, decoupaging furniture with photographs, stenciling shapes on fabric, sponging accents on bed rails, and more.

With all this talk of techniques, it may be dawning on you that it's been awhile since you've used a roller to cover a wall with paint or hung your own wallpaper border (or maybe all this is as new to you as diapers and baby monitors). If so, flip first to the book's Basic Techniques section, beginning on page 110. It's the just-the-facts overview you've been hoping for. We cover all you need to brush up on—or acquaint yourself with—painting, wallpapering, and surface decoration.

Finally, as you go back and face those blank walls and white shades and wonder where to begin, remember that the room's most important feature has nothing at all to do with paint colors, fabric patterns, and the rest. The best way to get started is to spend a little time with its living, breathing inhabitant, and go from there.

FIRST STEPS

1

No one needs to tell you that your child is a distinct little individual, complete with his or her very own preferences, aversions, habits, and interests. Combine what you know about those traits with a few basic truths about creating appealing and safe settings for kids, and you've got the foundation you need for making decorating decisions.

age

AFTER A CERTAIN AGE, YOUR CHILD WILL HAVE NO TROUBLE telling you exactly which parts of her room she feels she's outgrown. But even before she hits that stage, you can follow some general age guidelines. Newborns, for example, can't see well enough to appreciate much decorating detail. In fact, for their first six to nine months, they seldom respond to color. That's why many recommend decorating nurseries in a style that's soft, subtle—and soothing primarily to the parents who will spend many hours a day (and night) in the room. From the ages of about two to five, children become curious, climbing, poking adventurers. Furnishings need to be hard-wearing and safety proof. This is also the time when children become avid collectors of toys (think storage) and fans of story-book and cartoon characters (you may find yourself painting Winnie the Pooh on the walls). Cribs give way to beds at this stage, too. Kids who are six to eight begin hosting more friends in their rooms and developing stronger opinions about its decor. As they progress toward the late preteen years, they're typically interested in exchanging absolutely any decor they consider too young for posters, hobby accessories, and more grown-up furnishings. They're also in need of well-equipped study areas at this age.

ABOVE: Newborns can't see well enough to appreciate an elaborately decked-out nursery anyway, so why not create a calmer setting, one you'll find it relaxing to spend time in yourself.

size & scale

IF YOU WANT THEM TO HANG UP THEIR clothes, play contentedly, and put their toys away when they're finished, you obviously can't plunk your children down in the middle of rooms where everything is made for people twice their size. Try to make sure at least some of the coat hooks, clothing racks, drawers, and shelves in your child's room are at kid level. This not only gives him a sense of independence and you some peace (he doesn't have to yell for you every time he needs the blue bunny or his red jacket), but it allows him to begin developing responsibility for ordering and storing his own belongings. You might also consider outfitting the room with a few pieces of child-size furniture. A small table-and-chairs set is an especially good idea for young children who need a comfy place for creating works of art, hosting tea parties, and piecing together puzzles.

ABOVE: Child-size furniture gives young children a place to play that feels just right.

LEFT: Give your children access to some of their own stored belongings.

color

YOU MAY FEEL YOU NEED TO RESTRAIN YOURSELF IN THE REST of the house: pale yellow in the kitchen, a tasteful taupe in the living room. But kids' rooms are the place to celebrate the bold, boisterous colors children love and every inner child craves. Until the age of about 10, most kids are drawn to the visual stimulation of bright, pure colors, with the three primary hues—red, yellow, and blue—topping the popularity list. Even children who can't verbally express which colors they're most drawn to will offer you clues (the most-used Crayons in the box, for example, or the most-frequently chosen colors of construction paper). Get a

sense of your child's preferences, then splash them around liberally and in adventurous combinations. Sheets and pillow covers are a good place to play out color schemes; about the time your child decides she prefers solid lavender to bright red checks, the linens are probably looking a little worn anyway. Other ways to add a lot of color without a tremendous amount of work are to paint or paper one wall and leave the others neutral, train your paintbrush on the room's trim and small furniture pieces rather than on its major features, or purchase colorful but inexpensive accent pieces, such as small lampshades or throw pillows.

Young children respond especially well to bright, pure, primary colors. Don't be afraid to use them all at once.

flexibility

SCAN ANY OF THE PRECEDING SECTIONS, AND IT QUICKLY becomes clear. Unless you're prepared to spend a decade or so rewallpapering, repainting, and purchasing piece after piece of new furniture, you want furnishings and decor you can easily adapt to suit your child's changing needs. Look for furniture that can be raised, added onto, or reconfigured as a child grows—or that converts to other uses. Many furniture manufacturers sell modular groupings and convertible pieces for children's rooms, featuring everything from drawer units that can be stacked in different heights to cribs that convert into beds. When it comes to

wallpaper and paint, think in terms of accents rather than overhauls. Repainting the knobs on a neutral-colored dresser is a far easier way to carry out your child's new color scheme than repainting every piece of furniture in the room. And, when your little darling decides the dinosaurs on his wall simply must go, it's less of a job to change a wallpaper border than to strip and repaper all four walls.

ABOVE: These classic-looking storage cabinets that hold towels and baby toys today will look perfectly at home housing textbooks and sound system equipment several years from now.

safety

WHEN YOU'RE DECORATING, IT'S important to regularly view your child's room the way he or she does. Long, dangling cords are obviously meant for pulling and tugging, and furniture pieces that store enticing items in clear view way up high are clearly designed for climbing upon. Do this little exercise often enough, and you'll decide the only safe solution is to create a room for your child that resembles an unadorned padded cell. Before you do that, try some basic child-proofing tactics.

Don't let electrical cords dangle from tables or dressers. Use blinds and shades without looped cords. While you're at it, if the room is inhabited by a child of teething age, cover electrical cords with molded plastic covers.

Make sure cribs and all other furniture pieces are assembled properly and that they comply with consumer product safety standards. Cribs and beds for very young children need crib rails or bed rails.

Stop up all electrical outlets with safety plugs.

Install a smoke alarm in the room.

Put anti-skid mats under area rugs, and make sure carpeting is securely tacked down.

Anchor heavy furniture pieces to walls, and store heavy items in bookcases on bottom shelves.

Use window guards to restrict access through window openings.

Install doorknobs without locks.

2
WILD KINGDOMS

No need for them to know just yet what a jungle it can be out there. For now, let them reign over an empire of amiable creatures designed to decorate walls, dance across fabric, swing from strings, roll along floors, and provide general delight.

faux trophies

Think of these as hunting-lodge-style mounts for the tenderhearted. They're created using the most compassionate form of taxidermy ever: puppet stuffing. Start with purchased hand puppets of bucks, bears, or other big-game animals. Then follow our instructions for transforming them into clever wall mounts that keep friendly watch over all the goings-on below.

MATERIALS & TOOLS

- Animal hand puppet
- Polyester fiberfill stuffing
- Approximately 16 inches (40.6 cm) medium-gauge wire
- Small piece of foam core board
- Tape measure or ruler
- Craft knife
- Awl
- Fabric glue
- Nail or picture-hanging hook
- Hammer

INSTRUCTIONS

1. Trim off most of the length of your hand puppet's "neck."

2. Fold the wire in half, and stick it inside the head area, with the ends extending out of the neck opening. Stuff the head firmly with fiberfill. Make sure you stuff securely around the wire portion that's inside the head.

3. Measure the neck opening, and cut a piece of foam core board that will fit snugly into the opening. Use the awl to poke two holes in the foam core board for the wire ends.

4. Push the foam core board tightly into the remaining neck area. Pull the wires through the holes, and twist their ends together to make a loop.

5. Run a bead of fabric glue along the outer edges of the foam core board, then smooth the neck edge over it, pressing firmly. Let the glue dry.

6. Hook the looped wire over a nail or picture-hanging hook in the wall.

critter caddies

The members of this cuddly chorus line on wheels are multitalented. They roll anywhere you want them to go, look irresistibly cute in the process, and they'll hold nearly anything you ask them to—from books and toys to shoes and plastic game pieces—under their cushioned seat covers.

CADDIE BOX *step-by-step*

WHAT TO CUT

The simplest approach to this project is to purchase a 10-foot (3 m) length of 12-inch (30.5 cm) lumber from your local lumberyard or home center and cut it up. Generally you'll find that material sold as 12-inch (30.5 cm) lumber will actually measure 11½ inches (29.2 cm) wide. The actual finished width is not important as long as you note it and make your cover accordingly.

DESC.	QTY.	THICKNESS	WIDTH	LENGTH
sides	2	¾ inch (1.9 cm)	11½ inches (29.2 cm)	21½ inches (54.6 cm)
ends	2	¾ inch (1.9 m)	11½ inches (29.2 cm)	9 inches (22.9 cm)
bottom	1	¾ inch (1.9 cm)	10½ inches (26.7 cm)	21½ inches (54.6 cm)
lid	1	¾ inch (1.9 cm)	10½ inches (26.7 cm)	21½ inches (54.6 cm)
legs	4	Dowel Rod	2 inches (5.1 cm) dia.	2½ inches (6.4 cm)

NOTES: Cut your sides and ends first. You may need to slightly adjust the bottom and lid pieces based on the dimensions of the assembled sides and ends. Also, if you have difficulty locating 2-inch (5.1 cm) dowel rod, look for wooden closet hanger rod.

MATERIALS & TOOLS

- Acrylic paint
- Wood glue
- 8d ring shank nails (They make for strong assembly.)
- Four 1½-inch (3.8 cm) stem-type casters
- Continuous hinge (also known as a piano hinge), 24 x ¾ inches (61 x 1.9 cm)
- Sandpaper
- #6 round head screws, ⅝ inch (1.6 cm)
- Chain to support the open door
- Paintbrush
- Standard measuring tools
- Hammer
- Square
- Electric drill
- Compass
- Hacksaw
- Screwdriver

INSTRUCTIONS

1. Before putting your box together, paint the wood surfaces that will form the interior, and let them dry completely.

2. Assemble the sides and ends of the box by gluing the sides to the ends and then nailing the pieces together. After nailing, check your assembly with a square and adjust if necessary.

3. Using the actual outside dimensions of the assembly, cut your bottom and lid pieces to size. They should be the same.

4. Following the installation instructions for the casters you've selected, drill a hole the appropriate diameter and depth in the center of each dowel rod.

5. On the underside of the box bottom, locate four points 1½ inches (3.8 cm) in from both ends and sides. Set your compass for a 1-inch (2.5 cm) radius, and draw 2-inch (5.1 cm) circles, using these points as centers. Using glue and three nails for each, fasten the legs to the bottom of the box, with the circles serving as guides. Avoid nailing in the center of the legs, since this could interfere with the stem of your casters.

6. Attach the bottom of the box to the assembled sides and ends, using wood glue and nails around the perimeter and being certain to keep all the edges of the bottom flush with the sides.

7. Check your lid for fit. It should lie on top of the assembled box and be flush with all four sides. Before installing the hinge, cut it to length with a hacksaw. You want it approximately ½ inch (1.3 cm) shorter than the side where you're attaching it. Following the instructions and using the screws provided with the hinge, attach the lid. (Predrilling the screw holes makes this easier. The pre-drilled hole should be large enough to allow for easy assembly but not so large that the screws won't hold properly. It's a good idea to test your hole size in a scrap of wood first.)

8. Sand the entire assembly, easing the square edges slightly.

NOTE: You may find it easier to move on to the steps of covering your box (page 21) before installing the hardware and adding the casters.

9. Use the screws to attach the safety chain. Fasten one end to the inside of the front side of the box, approximately 1½ inches (3.8 cm) in from the end and 1 inch (2.5 cm) down from the top edge of that side. Fasten the other end to the box lid, 2¼ inches (5.7 cm) from the side edge and 1¾ inches (4.4 cm) down from the top edge. Adjust the length of the chain so that the lid will open a bit just past 90°. This will keep the lid open when in use. (Another option would be to use a toy box closure, which controls the rate at which a lid closes, thereby helping to prevent pinched fingers and banged heads. You can find toy box closures at most woodworking supply stores; they come with installation instructions.)

10. Mount the casters in the holes you drilled in the dowels.

MATERIALS & TOOLS

- ¾ yard (.66 m) of fabric, 60 inches (152.4 cm) wide (Fleece is a good choice.)
- ¾ yard (.66 m) thin cotton or polyester batting
- Mercerized cotton thread
- Fabric glue
- Polyester fiberfill
- Animal hand puppet
- Standard measuring and marking tools
- Scissors
- Straight pins
- Sharpened dowel rod
- Needle and thread for hand-sewing
- Sewing machine

FIGURE 1

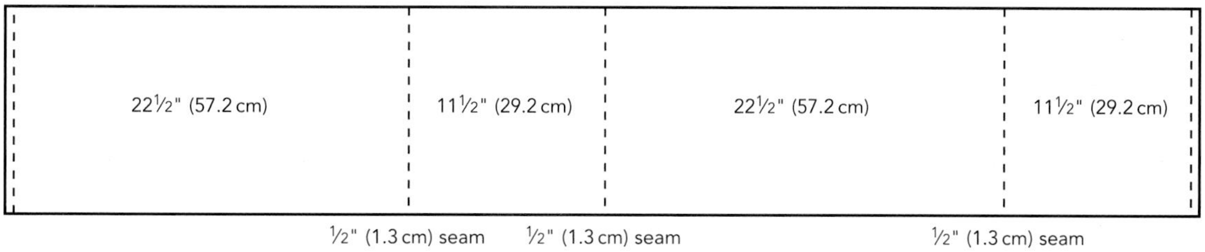

| 22½" (57.2 cm) | 11½" (29.2 cm) | 22½" (57.2 cm) | 11½" (29.2 cm) |

½" (1.3 cm) seam   ½" (1.3 cm) seam   ½" (1.3 cm) seam

FIGURE 2.
Fold the fabric diagonally at one corner.

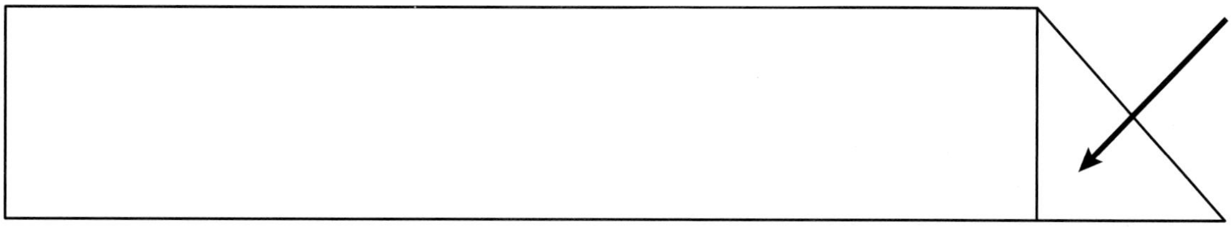

FIGURE 3

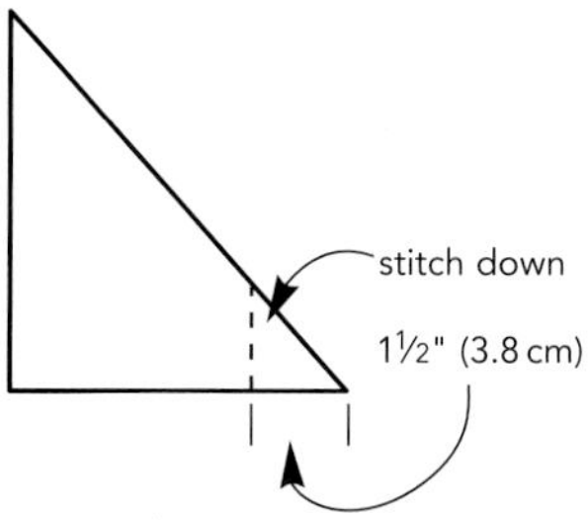

stitch down

1½" (3.8 cm)

INSTRUCTIONS

box sides

1. Cut two pieces of fabric 22½ x 12½ inches (57.2 x 31.8 cm) and two pieces 11½ x 12½ inches (29.2 x 31.8 cm).

2. Pin and sew one longer piece to one shorter piece at the shortest side, using a ½-inch (1.3 cm) seam allowance. Repeat with the other two pieces, then sew the two sewn pieces together on one short side, leaving the other side unsewn (see figure 1, page 21).

3. Cut a piece of batting 64 x 11½ inches (162.6 x 29.2 cm). Lay out the fabric piece, wrong side up, and place the batting on top of it, so there's a ½-inch (1.3 cm) border of fabric above and below the batting strip. Pin the batting in place.

4. Fold the fabric, right sides together, and stitch the remaining short side, catching the batting in the stitch.

5. To make top and bottom hems, fold ½ inch (1.3 cm) of fabric over the batting to the wrong side on both the top and bottom edges. Topstitch close to the folds. The finished size should be 11½ inches (29.2 cm).

6. Slip the piece over the box; it should fit snugly. Carefully run a bead of glue all around the top outside edge, one side at a time, and smooth the fabric over the glued area, pressing firmly. Repeat on the bottom edge.

covered top

1. Cut a piece of fabric 24 x 13 inches (61 x 33 cm), and make corner darts. With the right sides together, fold the fabric diagonally at one corner (see figure 2, page 21). Mark 1½ inches (3.8 cm) in from the corner point, and stitch down from this point (see figure 3, page 21). Repeat on the other three corners.

2. Cut a piece of batting 23 x 12 inches (58.4 x 30.5 cm). Make corner darts on this piece, following the directions in step 1, but marking the points only 1 inch (2.5 cm) in from the corners.

3. Place the batting on the wrong side of the fabric piece, fold the fabric edges over to cover the batting, and top-stitch close to the folded edge.

4. Place the piece over the top of the box. Run a bead of glue along the bottom edge of the outside of the box top, smooth the fabric over the glue, and press it firmly. Tie a wide piece of ribbon or scrap strip of fabric around the glued edge to give it added pressure until the glue dries completely.

legs

1. Measure around one of the legs, and cut four pieces of scrap fabric to fit.

2. Fold the raw edges of the pieces under, then glue them in place, pressing the fabric firmly.

head

Using a puppet is the simplest way to add a head to your caddie. However, if you're an experienced sewer, you could also use a commercially made animal pattern (or develop your own) to create the head yourself.

1. Trim off most of the length of your hand puppet's "neck."

2. Firmly stuff the head with fiberfill, using the dowel to push the stuffing into the head's outermost areas.

3. Turn the neck under a scant ¼ inch (6 mm). Slipstitch the head to one end of the box, taking tiny stitches to catch the fabric firmly.

mobiles

Infants spend much of the presitting, pre-toy-grasping stage of their lives lying in their cribs and looking up. What they'd *love* to see peering back at them every moment of the day and night, of course, is Mom's or Dad's face. But the next best thing, many exhausted parents have found, is a mobile made of interesting shapes that twist, twirl, cast shadows, catch light, and, most important, capture attention. Here are two variations that feature soft, friendly animals. One you make from scratch, the other you assemble using purchased stuffed toys.

MOBILE TIPS

■ A mobile frame should be constructed from a material that will support the suspended items without sagging. Circular frames can be constructed from foam core board, wire, wood, or premade circles such as embroidery hoops. Another common frame for a mobile features a series of short bars suspended from a larger central bar. Two crossed bars—made of wood, wire, or cardboard— also create an easy way to hang five shapes.

■ Hang your mobile well out of your infant's reach. No matter how well you think you've secured them, dangling items can come loose with a single tug.

■ Though small objects hanging from mobiles may be delightful for adults to look at, large objects are more suitable for babies. Not only are they easier to see, they can't be easily swallowed if they come loose. Babies' color vision doesn't mature until they're about four months old, so if you're making a mobile for a newborn, even black-and-white objects will keep him or her entertained.

■ Lightweight mobiles (such as the ones featured here) can be hung from a small screw hook. You can also hang them from a wire loop attached to a hollow wall anchor. If your mobile is heavy, hang it on a doorway frame or from a sturdy shelf.

MATERIALS & TOOLS

- Embroidered Animal Mobile patterns, page 120
- Scrap fabric remnants in solid colors
- Embroidery floss in contrasting colors
- 2 yards (1.8 m) small colored cording
- Polyester fiberfill for stuffing
- Mercerized cotton thread
- Large round wooden ring for attaching cord
- Fishing line
- Cup hook
- Scissors
- Standard measuring and marking tools
- Chalk pencil or water soluble marking pen
- Embroidery needle with a large enough eye to accommodate three strands of floss
- Small embroidery hoop
- Pencil
- Hand-sewing needle

FIGURE 1. Outline stitch

FIGURE 2. Making French knots

INSTRUCTIONS

1. Cut six 6-inch (15.2 cm) squares out of the scrap fabric.

2. Transfer the patterns on page 120 to the right side of the fabric using the chalk pencil or marking pen.

3. Center the embroidery hoop over one of your fabric squares. Thread the large-eyed needle with three strands of the same color of embroidery floss. Use an outline stitch (see figure 1) to hand-embroider all the solid lines. Make French knots (see figure 2) for the animals' eyes. Repeat the process on all the other fabric squares, using a different design on each.

4. Leaving a border of at least ¾ inch (1.9 cm) around all the edges, cut out the designs, and cut corresponding pieces for backing.

5. Cut the cord into six pieces of varying lengths. Pin one end of each cord to the right side of the top of an embroidered piece.

6. Pin together the embroidered pieces and backing pieces, right sides together. Using a ¼-inch (6 mm) seam allowance, stitch the pieces together, back tacking over the cord several times, and leaving a small opening (at least 1 inch [2.5 cm]) in the bottom edge, where you'll insert the stuffing. On each piece, be careful not to catch the cord in the seam; it should hang out through the opening at this point. Carefully clip just to the seam line along the curved edges, and turn the pieces right side out by pulling on the cord.

7. Use the eraser end of the pencil to push small bits of stuffing into the opening of each piece until it's plumply filled. Slipstitch the openings closed.

8. Tie the ends of the cords onto the round wooden ring, evenly spacing each piece.

9. Tie lengths of fishing line to two or three evenly spaced spots on the ring, knot the other ends together, and hang the knotted ends from a cup hook screwed securely into the ceiling.

Rather leave all the cutting and stitching to someone else? Here's a mobile variation made with the palm-sized stuffed animals so popular today. All it requires is some simple assembly.

1. Cut several-feet lengths of yarn or colored cording (about 1 meter), one length per stuffed animal. If you like, you can also wrap your mobile's wooden circle with the yarn or cord, then tie it off and clip the ends close.

2. Securely stitch one end of each piece of yarn or cord to the top of one animal head. Knot the yarn or cord to the wooden circle, so the animals hang several inches below it, then knot the other ends of the yarn or cord together.

3. Hang the knotted ends from a cup hook screwed securely into the ceiling.

stenciled menagerie

Admittedly, questions such as *When will I sleep again?* and *How will we pay for college?* probably top your lineup of parental concerns. But somewhere down the list is another: *What's the most efficient and economical way to use a design theme throughout my child's room?* We can help with the answer to this one: stencils. Better yet, we provide you with a whole menagerie of them on page 121, and give you instructions here for using them to create wooden toys and a printed quilt. Using the Basic Techniques, beginning on page 110, you could also easily paint them onto walls, floors, window trim, even furniture.

MATERIALS & TOOLS

- Stenciled Menagerie patterns, page 121
- Supply of blank acetate sheets
- Purchased blank quilt, comforter, or fabric throw (This technique won't be successful on a puffy piece of fabric; you want to work on fabric that is thin and firm, so the stencils will fit evenly on the surface.)
- Fabric paints in colors of your choice
- Fine-point permanent marking pen
- Craft knife
- Self-healing cutting mat or stack of magazines or newspapers
- Standard measuring and marking tools
- Masking tape
- Round stencil brushes (one for each color)
- Scrap cloth or paper
- Iron
- Pressing cloth

INSTRUCTIONS

1. Trace the patterns onto the blank acetate sheets, one pattern per sheet, using a permanent pen. You may want to use more than one color on a pattern, as we have here. If so, you'll need a different stencil for each color; trace as many copies of each pattern as you'll need.

2. Use a craft knife to cut out the darkened pieces of the stencils, working on a mat or a stack of newspapers or magazines. (Leave the acetate border around the patterns in place; it'll help protect your fabric when you apply the paint.)

3. Mark the spots on your quilt where you want your stenciled shapes.

4. Tape down all four sides of your first stencil on one of the spots you marked.

5. Dip the stencil brush into your first color of fabric paint, and dab it several times onto scrap cloth or paper (this is very important; if you use too much paint, it will seep under your stencil and make a mess). After blotting the brush well, dab paint onto your quilt through the stencil, applying it through only those areas where you want that color to appear. Start at the edges of the opening and continue toward the middle.

6. Carefully lift up the stencil (you don't want to smear paint), and tape it down on the next spot where you want that same shape and color to appear, and repeat the stenciling process. Continue moving the stencil until you've applied the first color through the first stencil shape everywhere you want it. Let the paint dry.

7. If you're adding another color to the same shape, grab your second stencil, align the stencil on top of the spot where you started stenciling, retape all four sides down, and add your second color through the appropriate openings.

8. Repeat the process to add other colors and to transfer the other stencil patterns.

9. When you're finished, thoroughly wash all your brushes in warm water, and allow them to dry.

10. Use the pressing cloth and iron to set the paint.

You can create these brightly painted animals to function as push or pull toys with wheels, as wall-hung decorations, or as accents you attach to otherwise plain furniture.

MATERIALS & TOOLS

- Stenciled Menagerie patterns, page 121
- Supply of blank acetate sheets
- Wood; enough to make the number of animals you want (Choose a good grade of Medium Density Fiberboard [MDF] or plywood. A wood thickness of ¾ inch [1.9 cm] is best for making toys; use ½-inch [1.3 cm] wood for decorative pieces.)
- Sandpaper
- Primer
- Acrylic paint in a variety of bright colors
- Masking tape
- Dowel rod for axles (optional) (Choose a diameter that matches that of the predrilled holes in your wheels.)
- Wheels (optional) (You can find inexpensive stock wheels for toys at craft stores. Wheels measuring 1½ to 2½ inches in diameter [3.8 to 6.4 cm] work well for most toys.)
- Wood glue
- Nylon cord (optional)

- Wooden beads, at least 1½ inches (3.8 cm) in diameter (optional)
- ⅜ inch (9.5 mm) dowel rods for push-toy handles (optional) (You'll want lengths of approximately 24 to 30 inches [61 to 76.2 cm] per toy.)
- Saw-toothed picture hangers (optional)
- Standard measuring tools
- Scissors
- Craft knife
- Cutting mat or stack of magazines or newspapers
- Scroll saw
- Electric drill
- Paintbrush
- Stencil brushes

INSTRUCTIONS

1. Enlarge the patterns to the size you want, then photocopy them onto a stencil material such as clear acetate.

2. Cut out the acetate animal shapes. Working on a cutting mat or a stack of magazines or newspapers, use a craft knife to also cut out the dark pieces inside the animal shape (to create stencil holes through which you'll later apply paint).

3. Use the acetate patterns to transfer the outline shapes of the animals to the wood.

4. Cut out the animal shapes with a scroll saw. Smooth the edges with sandpaper. (Use a high-quality scroll saw blade with 10 or 12 teeth per inch [2.5 cm], and you won't have to do much sanding of your edges.)

5. If you're making toys with wheels, drill axle holes in the feet area of the animals. The diameter of the holes you need will depend on the size of the dowel rods you've chosen for axles.

6. Prime each piece, then apply a base coat of color.

7. Tape the stencils in place on the pieces, and use stencil brushes to apply bright colors of paint through the stencil holes. Let the paint dry completely.

8. If you're attaching wheels, cut the dowel-rod axles to size. You want about ⅛-inch (3 mm) clearance between the wheel and the toy on each side. Use wood glue to secure the rod in the predrilled holes in the wheels.

9. To make pull toys, drill a small hole in the front end of each animal. String a length of cord through each hole, then knot a large wooden bead on the ends to create a handhold.

10. To make push toys, drill an angled hole ⅜ inch (9.5 mm) in diameter and about 1 inch (2.5 cm) deep somewhere along the edge of each toy. Use wood glue to secure a long dowel rod into each hole for a handle. Attach a large wooden bead to the other end of each dowel rod, again using wood glue. (Note: if you want to test your handle location and angle before drilling, temporarily attach the dowel rod with masking tape.)

11. To make wall decorations, attach saw-toothed picture hangers to the back of each animal.

12. If you want to use the pieces to decorate furniture, your mounting methods will vary. Something as simple as screws though the furniture member into the back of the piece will work in many cases. You can also fasten small wooden blocks to the back of the pieces. The blocks allow you to mount your pieces to the edges of shelves or furniture.

THE SUN MOON & STARS

No question about it. You'd move heaven and earth for them, and give your kids the sun, the moon, and the stars if they asked you to. Just in case they do, here's a chapter full of heavenly ideas you'll have no trouble bringing down to earth.

pick up
the pattern

Want a unified look that blends what you buy with what you do yourself? It's easy to pick up a design motif from a purchased piece (the moons and suns from a comforter or a wallpaper pattern, for example) and use it to add look-alike embellishment to another (such as the wooden bed canopy, shown here). Here's how to create your own stencil so you can transfer a pattern.

MATERIALS & TOOLS

- Fabric or paper with motif you want to replicate
- Photocopier
- Clear acetate
- Craft knife and several sharp blades
- Self-healing cutting mat or stack of newspapers or magazines to use as a cutting surface
- Masking tape

INSTRUCTIONS

1. Choose which motif(s) you want to use as a stencil. Select motifs that are not too detailed, or simplify a motif you really like. It's easiest if you choose a design with broad areas of one color. (You can add details later with a paint pen or brush.)

2. Photocopy your selected motif, enlarging or reducing it to suit your needs. Make several copies and set them aside. If your motif has details inside the central shape, the additional copies will serve as a handy reference.

3. Tape a photocopy to the self-healing cutting mat. Tape a sheet of the acetate on top of the copy. Begin by cutting any small, detached areas of the design—the rays of the sun in the project shown here, for example—with the craft knife. Be sure you have a very sharp blade in your craft knife and that you replace it often as you cut out your stencils. A dull blade will not give your stencil the crisp edges that you'll need for successful stenciling. Once you've cut out the small parts, cut out the central portion of the motif.

4. Your stencil is ready to use, but just to be on the safe side (and while you have the hang of it) cut out a second stencil. You may be happier with the result, and you'll have an additional stencil to use as one stencil dries. For general directions on stenciling, refer to page 116.

cloud cover

Bring a bit of the wild blue yonder indoors with a basic sponging technique for covering furniture, bedposts, walls, and, of course, ceilings with clouds. Whether you fill your skies with white billowy puffs, wispy streaks, or the promise of thunder and rain is entirely up to you—it's all in the flick of the wrist and the color of the paint on the sponge.

MATERIALS & TOOLS

- Light sky-blue latex or acrylic paint
- Various shades of white latex or acrylic paints: very light gray-white, very light blue-white, pure white (Purchase a pure-white paint and mix small amounts of a gray and light sky-blue paints to create these tones.)
- Paintbrush
- Newspaper
- Sea sponge
- Shallow containers such as disposable plates

INSTRUCTIONS

1. Paint your background sky blue. Let the first coat dry, then re-coat it if you like.

2. Pour a bit of the white paint into a shallow container. Blend in a little gray paint to create a gray-white. Lightly tap the sponge into the paint. Blot the sponge on the newspaper until it is almost dry. Begin to outline a cloud shape, using a light touch with the sponge. Fill in the shape using a light sponging touch. Let the shape dry a bit.

3. Pour a small amount of the white paint into another container. Blend in a tiny amount of the sky blue to create a blue-white tone. Again, tap the sponge into the paint and blot it. Sponge this color onto the clouds a little bit in from the edge, so the cloud has an edge of gray. Occasionally, allow the paint to extend over the gray edge for variety. Let the clouds dry completely.

4. Using the same sponging technique as in the previous steps, finish the clouds with a light coat of pure white. Sponge the paint a little bit in from the edges of the previously applied colors. Occasionally, extend the pure white over the edges. Let the paint dry.

shelf
shades

Here's another easy way to tie together a theme. Celestial-style sheets—just like the ones your little angel curls up under at night—can also mask clutter and, at the same time, help a set of utilitarian storage shelves get into the spirit of the room. Purchase an extra flat sheet or two when you buy the set for the bed, then follow our instructions for transforming them into roll-up shades with tassels.

MATERIALS & TOOLS

- Flat sheets (or decorator fabric) for the front of the shades (The amount you need will depend on the dimensions of your shelving unit. Add 1 inch [2.5 cm] to its width dimensions, and 5 inches (12.7 cm) to its height to determine what size sheet or how much fabric you need to buy.)

- Flat sheets (or decorator fabric) in a contrasting design for the lining (same as the amount you need for the facing)

- 2¾ yards (2.5 m) sew-on hook-and-loop tape

- 14 double tassels

- 4 yards (3.6 m) small decorator cord in a color that coordinates with the tassels

- Mercerized cotton thread

- Upholstery weight thread and large needle

- Standard measuring and marking tools

- Scissors

- Iron

- Sewing machine

- Hammer (optional)

- Small nails (optional)

INSTRUCTIONS

1. Measure and cut the sheets you've chosen for the front of the shades. You need pieces that are the right dimensions for covering all of your shelf unit's openings. In addition, you need to add approximately 5 inches (12.7 cm) to the length of each piece, so you can attach the shades by wrapping them over your shelf unit's top bar (see step 3). If your shelf unit doesn't have a top bar, don't add the 5 inches (12.7 cm). Cut identical pieces out of the sheets you're using for the lining.

2. Lay out your fabric and pin the lining pieces to the front pieces, right sides together. Stitch the fronts and linings together, using a ½-inch (1.3 cm) seam allowance and leaving a 6-inch (15.2 cm) opening at the bottom edge of each piece. Turn the pieces right side out through the openings, press them, and topstitch close to the edge on all four sides of each piece.

3. Cut hook-and-loop tape to fit along the top edges of all of your pieces. Sew one side of the tape to the lining side of the top edges. If your shelf unit has a top bar, drape the top edge of your pieces over the bar, mark the point where the draped-over edge hits the lining, and sew the other side of the tape to the lining, along the mark. (The top edge of the fabric creates a casing that surrounds the bar and seals itself off with the hook-and-loop tape.) If your shelf unit doesn't have a top bar, nail the other side of the hook-and-loop tape to the front edge of the top shelf.

4. For the top row of tassels, equally space the tassels in (approximately 4 to 6 inches [10.2 to 15.2 cm]) from the side edges of each shade and down (approximately 12 inches [30.5 cm]) from the top edge. Also, center a tassel on the front shade. Use upholstery weight thread and a large needle to securely hand-sew the tassels in place. When you hand-sew the tassels in place, simultaneously sew 8-inch (20.3 cm) loops of coordinating cord to the lining piece, directly behind the tassels.

5. Add a lower row of tassels and loops of cord where you want them, lining them up with the tassels on the top row.

6. Attach the shades. When you want to roll them up, bring the tassels through the loops to hold the rolled shades in place.

WINDOW SHADE *variation*

If you want window shades rather than (or in addition to) shelf shades, measure your window openings, add 1 inch (2.5 cm) to the width and 4 inches (10.2 cm) to the length, then create your shades in the same way. Instead of using hook-and-loop tape to attach them, simply sew a narrow curtain-rod casing along the top edge of your shades.

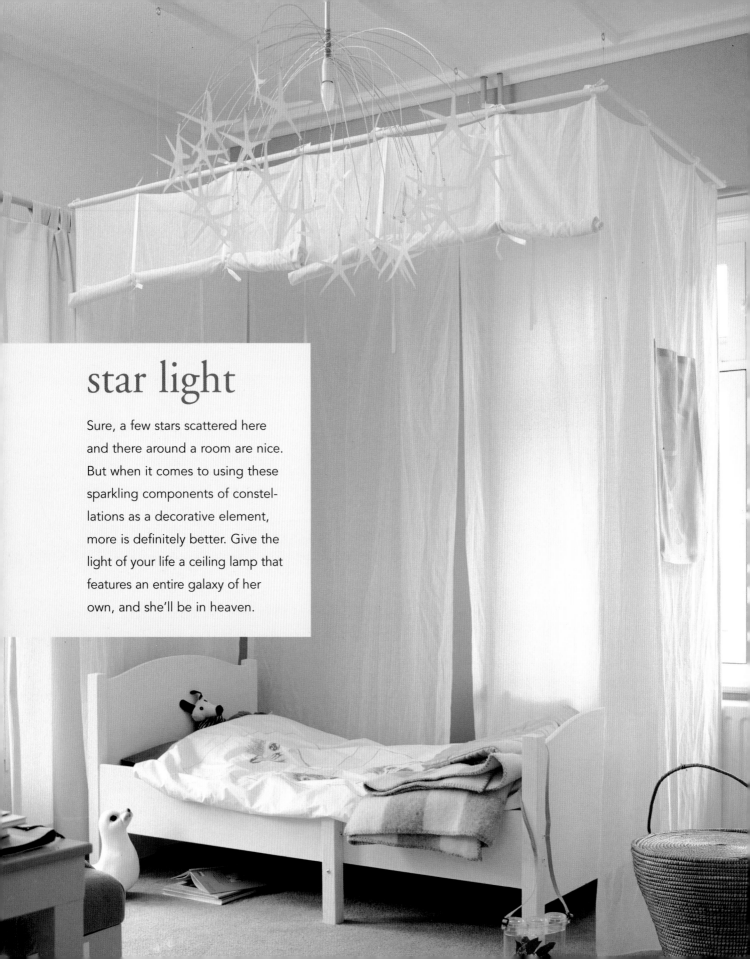

star light

Sure, a few stars scattered here and there around a room are nice. But when it comes to using these sparkling components of constellations as a decorative element, more is definitely better. Give the light of your life a ceiling lamp that features an entire galaxy of her own, and she'll be in heaven.

MATERIALS & TOOLS

■ You'll find much of what you need for this project at a home improvement store; head to the electrical section for most of the materials. If you don't want to make 40 stars yourself, you can substitute the glow-in-the-dark star shapes sold at craft and toy stores.

■ Star Light pattern, page 122

■ .080 clear acrylic sheet

■ Pendant light fixture (These are sometimes called warehouse lights. They have a single cord and a wide, metal shade. Look for a fixture with a removable shade.)

■ 14 stranded white-coated electrical wire, cut into lengths ranging from 24 to 36 inches (61 to 92 cm)

■ 1 candle-shaped bulb

■ Fine-grit abrasive paper or sanding sponge

■ Pencil

■ Jigsaw or motorized cutting tool with a cutting blade

■ Drill and small drill bit

■ Wire cutters

■ Pliers

INSTRUCTIONS

This project involves installing an electrical fixture, which is not as daunting as you might think. But if you're wary, hire an electrician or coax an electrically savvy friend into hanging the light for you.

1. Scrub both sides of the acrylic sheet with the abrasive paper or sanding sponge to give the acrylic a frosted finish.

2. Use a photocopier to enlarge the star pattern to about 6 inches (15.2 cm) from point to point.

3. Lay the pattern under the acrylic sheet and trace the shape with the pencil. You will need 40 stars for this lamp.

4. Use the jigsaw or motorized cutting tool to cut out all 40 shapes.

5. Make a mark on one point of each star. Drill holes at the marks.

6. Wire and hang the pendant lamp without the shade. Be sure you turn off the correct circuit at the circuit box before doing so.

7. Make a small hook on each end of a length of the stranded wire. Slip the hook into a hole in a star. Twist the wire to secure the shape. Use pliers if necessary to secure the twist. Repeat until you've attached all of the stars to wires.

8. Take two strands in hand, and place them on either side of the pendant lamp wire hanging from the ceiling. Twist the wires together a couple of times on either side of the central wire. Continue adding pairs of wires in the same manner. You'll be able to arrange the stars by rotating the twisted wires.

crib canopy

Lull your little one into slumber anytime with the help of this breezy night sky. A strip of fabric, some simple-to-cut felt celestial shapes, and the easy suspension system we describe here are all you need. Fortunately, you've already got the center of the universe.

MATERIALS & TOOLS

- 4½ yards (4.1 m) cotton duck fabric or canvas
- Mercerized cotton thread
- Felt squares in various colors
- Fabric glue
- 4 cup hooks
- Two 30-inch (76.2 cm) dowel rods
- Fishing line
- Standard measuring and marking tools
- Scissors
- Iron
- Sewing machine

INSTRUCTIONS

1. Cut your fabric into a piece 32 inches (81.3 cm) wide by the piece's full length. Press the edges of all the sides under 1 inch (2.5 cm), then press and fold again inside the folded edge to create a finished ½-inch (1.3 cm) double hem. Stitch close to the folded edge.

2. Cut out star shapes (or other celestial shapes) from felt. Randomly affix them with glue to the canopy, gluing them only at their centers.

3. Screw the cup hooks into the ceiling directly above the four corners of the crib.

4. Tie the fishing line securely around the ends of the dowels, then hang the dowels from the hooks.

5. Drape the canopy over the dowels with a slight sway in the middle. The felt shapes should be facing down toward the crib.

SECRET GARDENS

4

Stitch bright blossoms, create papier-mâché petals, and paint a few delicate blooms. All are easy ways to give your budding young things their own patches of paradise—spots where they can't help but thrive and grow.

soft-sculpture flowers & pots

These lively floral bunches are toys, throw pillows, and decorative accents all in one. Toss a bouquet on top of a bright bedspread, prop a cluster in a painted pot, or stand a line of single blooms along the windowsill.

MATERIALS & TOOLS

- Flower patterns, page 122
- All-cotton fabric in a selection of colors and patterns: terra-cotta pots, ½ yard (.45 m) per pot; pots with handles, ¼ yard (.23 m) of outer fabric and ¼ yard (.23 m) of lining per pot; flowers, scrap fabric remnants
- Polyester batting, ¼ inch (6 mm) thickness
- Mercerized cotton thread in colors that coordinate with your fabric
- Embroidery floss in various colors
- Polyester stuffing
- Standard measuring and marking tools
- Scissors
- Large-eyed needle
- Bodkin (a tweezer-like tool that helps with turning)
- Small dowel or pencil
- Sewing machine

INSTRUCTIONS

Terra-cotta Pots

1. Cut two pieces of fabric measuring 18 x 9 inches (45.7 x 22.9 cm) and two 6-inch (15.2 cm) circles.

2. Lay one of the fabric rectangles out flat, mark in 1 inch (2.5 cm) from the bottom side edges. Using a straightedge, draw a line from this mark to the upper edges, so your pot will have a tapered shape (see figure 1). Trim the fabric along these lines.

FIGURE 1

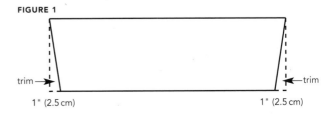

trim → ← trim
1" (2.5 cm)   1" (2.5 cm)

3. Lay the trimmed piece on top of the other rectangle, and trim the second one to the same size.

4. To create the outer pot, lay one of the trimmed rectangles on a piece of polyester batting, and trim the batting to size. Pin the batting to the wrong side of the fabric. Roll the piece into a tube shape, with the right sides of the fabric together and bringing the short ends together. Stitch along those short ends, using a ½-inch (1.3 cm) seam allowance. To hold the batting in place along the bottom edge and for clipping purposes later, stitch ½ inch (1.3 cm) in from the bottom raw edge.

5. For the lining of the pot, pin the other trimmed rectangle together just as you did for the outer pot (but without the batting), and stitch it along the sides.

6. Cut one 5-inch (12.7 cm) circle from the batting. Place it on the wrong side of one of the 6-inch (15.2 cm) fabric circles, leaving ½ inch (1.3 cm) all the way around for a seam. Using a long basting stitch on the machine, stitch ¾ inch (1.9 cm) in from the edges to hold the batting in place. Pin the other fabric circle over the batting (right sides facing out on both fabric circles), and machine baste again along a ½-inch (1.3 cm) seam line.

7. With the wrong (batting) side of the outer pot piece facing out and the right sides together, pin the bottom piece to the outer pot piece. Clip just to the stitching line to ease in the fullness (see figure 2). Stitch, using a ½-inch (1.3 cm) seam allowance.

8. Pin the lining piece to the outer pot piece, right sides together and matching the seam lines. Stitch the pieces together along the upper edge, using a ½-inch (1.3 cm) seam allowance. Pull the lining piece out, smooth it over the batting side of the outer pot, and hand-sew it to the seam line of the bottom of the pot, making sure the raw edge is covered by the lining. Turn the pot right side out.

9. Using three strands of embroidery floss and the large-eyed needle, make straight stitches along the top edge of the pot (using the project photo as a guide). Fold the top edge over to the outside approximately 2 inches (5.1 cm) to form a lip for the pot.

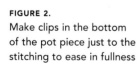

FIGURE 2.
Make clips in the bottom of the pot piece just to the stitching to ease in fullness

Pot with Handles

1. Cut two pieces from the outer fabric, each measuring 10 x 9 inches (25.4 x 22.9 cm). Cut two pieces with the same dimensions out of the lining fabric. Also out of outer fabric, cut four C-shaped pieces approximately 3 inches (7.6 cm) tall for handles (see figure 3), and two 6-inch (15.2 cm) circles.

2. If you like, hand-sew decorative patches of fabric randomly placed on one of the rectangles of outer fabric, using embroidery floss and long stitches.

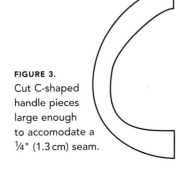

FIGURE 3.
Cut C-shaped handle pieces large enough to accomodate a ¼" (1.3 cm) seam.

3. Lay out one piece of outer fabric, make a mark 1 inch (2.5 cm) in from the bottom side edges, and draw straight lines to the upper side edges (as you did in step 1 for the Terra-cotta Pot). Trim along these lines. Use the trimmed pieces to mark and trim identical strips on the other piece of outer fabric and on the lining pieces.

4. Create the handles by sewing two C-shaped pieces together, right sides together, leaving the ends open for turning and stuffing. Use the bodkin to turn the piece right side out and the eraser end of a pencil to stuff it with small bits of stuffing until it's firm. Leave ½ inch (1.3 cm) unstuffed at each end. Pin and stitch one handle to each long edge of one of the outer pot pieces. (Use the project photo as a placement guide.)

5. Pin the batting piece to the wrong side of one of the outer pot pieces, and machine baste it in place along the side edges. Stitch ½ inch (1.3 cm) in from the bottom edge to hold the batting in place there and to create a clipping line for later.

6. Pin the two sides, right sides together, and stitch along both sides using a ½-inch (1.3 cm) seam allowance.

7. Cut one 5-inch (12.7 cm) circle from the batting. Place it on the wrong side of one of the 6-inch (15.2 cm) fabric circles, leaving ½ inch (1.3 cm) all the way around for a seam. Using a long basting stitch on the machine, stitch ¾ inch (1.9 cm) in from the edges to hold the batting in place. Pin the other fabric circle over the batting (right sides facing out on both fabric circles), and machine baste again along a ½-inch (1.3 cm) seam line.

8. With the wrong (batting) side of the outer pot piece facing out and the right sides together, pin the bottom piece to the outer pot piece, clipping just to the stitching line to ease in the fullness. Stitch, using a ½-inch (1.3 cm) seam allowance (again, see figure 2, page 42).

9. Sew the two lining pieces together along the sides, using a ½-inch (1.3 cm) seam allowance. Pin the lining piece to the outer pot piece, right sides together and matching the seam lines. Stitch the pieces together along the upper edge, using a ½-inch (1.3 cm) seam allowance. Pull the lining piece out, smooth it over the batting side of the outer pot, and hand-sew it to the seam line of the bottom of the pot, making sure the raw edge is covered by the lining. Turn the pot right side out.

Flowers

1. Enlarge the patterns on page 122 to the size you want. Add ¼ inch (6 mm) to the perimeters for a seam allowance, and cut flower heads out of colorful fabrics, and stems and leaves out of green fabrics.

2. Using the project photo as a guide, mark embroidery lines using a chalk pencil or water soluble pen. Using three strands of embroidery floss and a large-eyed needle, embroider the markings with straight stitches or French knots (see page 24).

3. For the flower heads, pin back pieces to front pieces, right sides together, and stitch them together, using a ¼-inch (6 mm) seam allowance and your tiniest machine stitch, and pivoting at the inner corners. Leave an opening at the bottom edge of each head, large enough to slip the stem into.

4. Clip just to the stitching line at curves and inner corners. Turn the heads, using a sharpened dowel or the eraser end of a pencil to push out all the petal points. Continue to use the dowel or pencil to push small bits of stuffing into the flower. Firmly fill the outermost areas first, then the centers.

5. Stitch leaves to the flower stems at the designated points, using a ¼-inch (6 mm) seam allowance.

6. Mark embroidery lines using a chalk pencil or a water soluble pen. Using three strands of embroidery floss and a large- eyed needle, make straight running stitches where indicated.

7. Pin the front and back pieces of the stems with leaves, right sides together, and stitch them, using a ¼-inch (6 mm) seam allowance and your tiniest machine stitch, and pivoting at the inner corners. Leave the bottom edge of each stem open.

8. Clip to the stitching line along curves and inner corners. Turn and stuff the leaves and stems firmly, using the dowel or pencil.

9. For each flower, insert the top of a stem (approximately ½ inch [1.3 cm]) into the bottom of a flower head through the opening you left. Slipstitch around the connection point, using tiny hand stitches.

floral photo transfers

Gardening magazines, seed packets, and perhaps even your own photo albums are bursting with brilliant color images of flowers in full bloom. To transfer those images to chair seats, mobile pieces, or numerous other flat surfaces, grab a good pair of scissors and follow along.

FLORAL PHOTO MOBILE *step-by-step*

MATERIALS & TOOLS

- 1 sheet of foam core board
- Floral images (from magazines, calendars, etc.)
- Spray mount
- Acrylic paint in color(s) of your choice
- Yarn (Choose a color to match the paint you've selected.)
- Clear nail polish
- Screw hook
- Ruler
- Pencil
- Craft knife
- Scissors
- Sandpaper
- Pot lid or large circular platter to use as a template. (Your circle should be at least 12 inches [30.5 cm] in diameter or larger.)
- Small paintbrush
- Awl
- Tapestry needle

INSTRUCTIONS

1. Measure and mark a square on the foam core board about 18 inches (45.7 cm) square. Cut it out with the craft knife. Set it aside.

2. Select eight similarly sized images with simple outlines that aren't too detailed. Trim the images with the scissors, leaving a border of approximately ½ inch (1.3 cm) all around. Set them aside.

3. Follow the manufacturer's instructions for applying the spray mount to the larger piece of foam core board (not the piece you set aside in step 1) and the back of the trimmed images. Lay one edge of an image on the board and carefully adhere the image, using your finger to smooth out any wrinkles that appear. Mount all of the images in the same way. Let them dry.

4. Use the craft knife to cut out the foam-core-backed images, trimming the excess border from the images as you go. If necessary, use the sandpaper to lightly sand the edges of the foam core board. Set the pieces aside.

5. Using the pot lid or large circular platter as a template, trace a large circle onto the square of board you set aside in step 1. Use the ruler and pencil to measure and mark 2 inches (5.1 cm) in from the edge of the circle. Make several of these marks around the inside of the circle, then connect them, so you end up with an inner circle.

6. Use the craft knife to cut out the outer circle, then the inner circle, so you end up with a 2-inch-wide (5.1 cm) ring. If necessary, use the sandpaper to smooth the inner and outer edges of the ring.

7. Use the small paintbrush to apply a coat of acrylic paint to both sides and all edges of the foam core ring. Let the paint dry.

8. Paint the back and edges of the mounted images. Let them dry.

9. Decide how you want your images to hang. Mark the top ends on the edges of the foam core. Set the images aside.

10. Measure and cut eight lengths of yarn, each measuring 48 inches (121.9 cm) long. Set them aside.

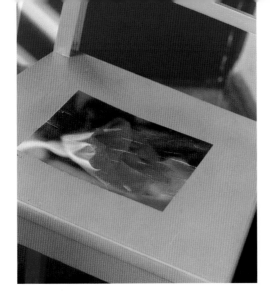

11. Picture the foam core ring as a clock face. Mark points at 12, 3, 6, and 9 o'clock. Then, make marks halfway between each of those four marks. Pierce each of the eight marks with the awl through to the opposite side.

12. Pierce the marks you made in step 9 with the awl, then widen them slightly.

13. Thread the tapestry needle with a length of yarn. Use the needle to pull the yarn through the hole you pierced in the top of one of the images. Leave a small tail, then tie the yarn securely to hang the image. If you like, apply a small amount of clear nail polish to secure the knot. Repeat the process with all the images.

14. Make an overhand knot about 12 inches (30.5 cm) above one image. Thread the needle with the free end of the yarn, and bring the thread up through the bottom of the foam core ring. Repeat this process on a second image, positioning it directly opposite on the ring.

15. Repeat step 14 with the remaining images, but vary the height at which you place the knot before you thread the image through the ring. As you thread each image, you'll be able to adjust the balance of the mobile by gathering the ends of the threads together and holding it at arm's length.

16. Balance the mobile, and pinch together the yarn about 18 inches (45.7 cm) above the ring. Tie the bundle of yarn together with a simple overhand knot. Secure the knot with a coating of clear nail polish.

17. Hang the mobile—well out of baby's reach—on a small screw hook.

MATERIALS & TOOLS

- Chair, sanded smooth and painted
- Floral images (from magazines, calendars, etc.)
- Scissors
- Spray fixative
- Wax paper
- Acrylic varnish, matte or glossy
- Paintbrushes
- Straight pins
- Polyurethane
- Fine grit wet/dry abrasive paper

INSTRUCTIONS

1. Trim the image you've selected to size.

2. Spray the front side of the image with a light coat of the fixative. Let it dry, and then repeat on the back of the image. This will prevent colors from running or the image on the reverse side of your selected image from bleeding through when you glue the image you've chosen to the chair.

3. Lay your image facedown on a length of wax paper. Coat the back of the image with the acrylic varnish.

4. Lift the image by the corners and carefully place it on the chair seat. Gently tug on the image and smooth out any large wrinkles with your fingers, then smooth the image onto the chair with a paintbrush lightly loaded with varnish. If any bubbles pop up, prick them with a straight pin, and then pat them flat with the brush. Let the image dry.

5. After the image is dry, re-coat the image with a light coating of varnish. Let it dry.

6. Finish the chair with two coats of polyurethane, lightly sanding in between coats.

gardener's corner

Like a little in-room potting shed, this cheerful nook is the perfect place for cultivating all kinds of talents. Assemble all the elements in one spot, as we have here, or simply pick a single project and add it to your own garden-room setting.

WALL SLOTS *step-by-step*

Fill these handy fabric pouches with books, art supplies, and a stuffed toy or two.

MATERIALS & TOOLS

- Appliqué patterns, page 123
- 2⅓ yards (2.1 m) sturdy fabric, such as cotton duck or lightweight canvas
- Strong (upholstery weight) thread
- Selection of all-cotton fabrics for appliqués
- 2 yards (1.8 m) fusible webbing
- Mercerized cotton thread in colors that coordinate with appliqué fabrics
- 10 small buttons to be covered with fabric (Typically sold as a package.)
- 2 plastic ring hangers
- 2 cup hooks
- Flat piece of wood, 48 x 2 inches (121.9 x 5.1 cm)
- Standard measuring and marking tools
- Scissors
- Iron
- Sewing machine with a strong shank needle
- Chalk pencil or water soluble marking pen
- Permanent marking pen

INSTRUCTIONS

1. Cut a piece measuring 54 x 56 inches (137.2 x 142.2 cm) out of the sturdy fabric. On the two shorter and one of the longer sides, turn back the fabric 3 inches (7.6 cm), then fold again inside the folded edge for a finished hem of 1½ inches (3.8 cm). Press the hem, and machine stitch it close to the folded edge using upholstery-weight thread and a strong shank needle.

2. For the top casing, turn the edge back 5 inches (12.7 cm), then fold inside the edge again for a doubled 2½-inch (6.4 cm) casing. Press and stitch the casing close to the folded edge.

3. Cut the following pieces out of sturdy fabric for the pockets: one 16 x 18 inches (40.6 x 45.7 cm), one 18 x 18 inches (45.7 x 45.7 cm), one 16 x 14 inches (40.6 x 35.6 cm), and three 10 x 10 inches (25.4 x 25.4 cm). Turn each under 1 inch (2.5 cm) on all four sides, then turn the folds under again, and press them. Stitch across tops only of each.

4. For appliqués, enlarge the patterns on page 123 to the size you want. Apply fusible webbing to the backs of the cotton pieces you've chosen for the appliqués, following the manufacturer's instructions. Using a chalk pencil or a marking pen, trace the patterns onto the right sides of the pieces, and cut out the shapes.

5. Lay all the appliqué pieces that don't go on top of pockets onto the wall hanging, using the photo as a placement guide. Follow the manufacturer's instructions to fuse the appliqués to the wall hanging. Do the same for the appliqués that go on top of pocket pieces. Stitch around the edges of all the pieces, using a zigzag stitch on the sewing machine with coordinating thread colors.

6. Cover the buttons, according to the directions on the package. Hand-sew them in place as accents on the wall hanging (again, using the photo as a guide for placement).

7. To define the sides of each pocket, fold back 1 inch (2.5 cm) on each side from the double-folded hem, and topstitch very closely to the folded-back edge.

8. Place the pockets on the wall hanging. Stitch the sides to the wall hanging. Tuck in the sides at the bottom edge (to give the pocket depth), and stitch the bottom close to the folded edge (see figure 1).

9. Using the permanent marking pen, draw lines for the snail and butterfly antennae, bee "trails," bee wings, and eyes, using the photo as a guide.

10. Sew one plastic ring to each of the top corners of the wall hanging, and screw cup hooks into the wall where you want your wall slots to hang.

11. Insert the wood in its casing, and mount your wall slots.

FIGURE 1

stitch sides to wall hanging

tuck the sides at the bottom and stitch close to the folded edge

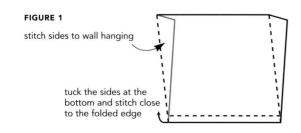

These fanciful organizers are perfect for a preschooler's work table—and an easy project for kids to help with.

MATERIALS & TOOLS

- Terra-cotta flowerpots
- Small paintbrushes
- Acrylic paints in white, green, pink, yellow, and blue
- Pencil

INSTRUCTIONS

1. Paint the insides and outsides of the pots with the white paint. Let the paint dry, then give the pots a second coat of paint. Add a third coat if you like.

2. Lightly sketch snails, flowers, or butterflies on each pot. You can use one motif per pot or mix them.

3. Choose a color for each motif—yellow butterfly wings, blue snail shells, and so on—and paint them. Let the paint dry.

4. Use contrasting colors to paint the details: antennae, body, plant stems, etc. Let them dry.

gardener's corner chair treatments

Create painted or padded garden-style chairs—or live it up and make both.

MATERIALS & TOOLS

- Painted Chair patterns, page 125
- Wooden chair
- Kraft paper
- Scrap piece of ¼-inch (6 mm) plywood
- Semi-gloss latex paint in red, yellow, and orange and/or light-colored wood stain in green or yellow
- Finish nails
- Wood putty
- Latex primer
- Low-tack painter's tape, 2-inch (5.1 cm) width
- Acrylic craft paints in red, yellow, green, and white (for mixing)
- Spray acrylic sealer or varnish
- Framing square or straightedge ruler
- Pencil
- Scissors
- Scroll saw or jigsaw
- Sandpaper
- Paintbrush or foam brush
- Clean rags
- Hammer
- Nail set
- Round decorative artist's brush

INSTRUCTIONS

Creating Wooden Embellishments

1. Measure the back and seat of your chair. Either enlarge the patterns for the headboard, back brace, and skirt on page 125 to the size you need, or use them as guides to create your own embellishment patterns. Transfer the patterns to kraft paper to create templates.

2. Lay the templates on the plywood, and trace around them to transfer the patterns to the wood. Use the scroll or jigsaw to cut out the embellishments, then sand around the edges and over the surfaces until they're smooth.

Painting the Chair and Embellishments

1. Make sure all your surfaces are free of dust and grime.

2. You may want to use colored stains on certain areas (the legs and back bars, for instance) and paint on the rest of the chair to create subtle textural differences. If so, apply your stain to the clean wood now, using a rag to wipe away the excess.

3. Use a hammer and finish nails to attach the embellishments to the chair. Set the nails, then fill the holes with wood putty. When the putty is dry, sand those areas lightly.

4. Prime all areas to be painted.

5. Use the red paint to cover the headboard, yellow for the seat and back brace, and orange for the skirting. You may need to apply two coats for solid coverage.

6. Use painter's tape to mask off a square in the center of the seat. Paint a red border around the taped square. Allow it to dry.

7. Practice making strokes with a round decorative brush before painting the flower accents on your chair. Press the fully loaded brush onto the surface. Pull the stroke toward you, gradually releasing the pressure. Allow the stroke to trail off, then lift your brush cleanly. Each stroke becomes the petal of a flower. Repeat this stroke, laying one petal next to the other in a circular pattern, creating the flower's head. When you're finished practicing, use yellow craft paint to create the flower on the headboard of the chair and red to create the flower centered in the square on the seat. Mix a little white paint with the yellow or red to create the color for the flowers' centers. Use a clean and dry brush to fill in the color in the center of the flowers. Use some of this color to also create highlights on the petals, applying it in small light strokes. Paint a stem for each flower with the green acrylic paint.

8. When all the paint is thoroughly dry, either spray clear acrylic sealer over the chair to protect it, or use a coat or two of varnish for a more durable finish.

MATERIALS & TOOLS

- Chair
- Newspaper
- ⅝ yard (.56 m) fabric for seat cover
- Mercerized cotton thread
- Scrap of all-cotton fabric for appliqué
- Fusible webbing
- 1½ yards (1.4 m) covered piping in a contrasting color
- 1 yard (.9 m) ribbon
- Standard measuring and marking tools
- Scissors
- Straight pins
- Sewing machine with zipper-foot attachment
- Iron
- Chalk pencil or water soluble marking pen
- Hand-sewing needle

INSTRUCTIONS

1. Trace your chair seat onto newspaper to create a paper pattern (see figure 1). Add ½ inch (1.3 cm) all the way around your pattern and draw a second outline of the pattern at this point. Cut out the pattern along the second outline, pin it on top of your fabric, and cut it out (see figure 2). For the skirt, cut one piece measuring 8 x 36 inches (20.3 x 91.4 cm) and another measuring 8 x 11 inches (20.3 x 27.9 cm).

2. Stay stitch around the perimeter of the seat cover ½ inch (1.3 cm) in from the raw edge, using your smallest machine stitch, and pivoting at the corners. Clip to the corners (see figure 3), and finish the edges around these corners by pressing under ½ inch (1.3 cm) to the wrong side, then pressing and folding again and stitching close to the fold, creating a finished ¼-inch (6 mm) hem at the corners.

3. Choose an appliqué shape from the Wall Slots project (page 49) to decorate the center of the seat cover. Enlarge the pattern (page 123) to the size you want. Apply fusible webbing to the back of the scrap of cotton fabric, following the manufacturer's instructions. Using a chalk pencil or a marking pen, trace the pattern onto the right side of the piece, and cut out the shape. Follow the manufacturer's instructions to fuse the appliqué to the seat cover, then stitch around the edges of the piece using a zigzag stitch on the sewing machine with coordinating thread colors.

4. Pin the covered piping to the edge of the seat cover along the line you stitched in step 2. Fold back the raw edge of the piping as you start pinning and as you finish. Place another piece of piping along the back edge of the seat cover along the stitched line. Stitch the piping in place, using a zipper-foot attachment (see figure 4).

5. Fold the longer skirt piece in half long ways, right sides together, so you end up with a piece measuring 4 x 36 inches (10.2 x 91.4 cm). Stitch across each short side, using a ½-inch (1.3 cm) seam allowance. Turn the piece right side out, press it, and stay stitch, using a ½-inch (1.3 cm) seam allowance, across the long edge. Repeat the process with the shorter skirt piece.

6. Pin the long skirt piece to the sides and front of the seat cover, right sides together, so the raw edges are even and the finished sides start at the beginning of the piping (see figure 5). At each front corner curve, clip to the stay-stitching line to ease the curves. Stitch the piece in place close to the piping edge, using a zipper-foot attachment. Repeat the process to stitch the shorter skirt piece to the back of the seat cover. Press the seams toward the seat cover.

7. Hand-stitch approximately 9 inches (22.9 cm) of ribbon trim to the side and back edges of the seat cover so you can tie it onto your chair.

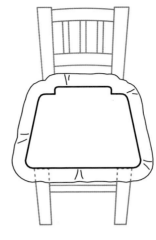

FIGURE 1.
Trace your chair seat onto newspaper to create a pattern.

FIGURE 2.
Cut out your pattern along the second outline.

FIGURE 3.
Clip to the corners, and finish the edges around those corners.

FIGURE 4.
Stitch the piping in place.

FIGURE 5.
Pin the skirt to the sides and front.

repetition, repetition, repetition

She likes—no, she loves—flowers. A lot. Why spend your energy trying to convince her that a few solid-color surfaces might also be nice, when it's so easy to cover every piece in sight with the petals and little green leaves she adores?

FLOWER POWER CUPBOARD *step-by-step*

MATERIALS & TOOLS

- Purchased unfinished wooden cupboard
- Acrylic paint
- Plastic container or jar
- Flower-patterned paper (Tissue paper, wallpaper, or specialty papers are all suitable.)
- Acrylic medium or lightly thinned white craft glue
- Polyurethane (optional)
- 2 large, wooden craft beads
- ¼ yard (.23 m) of patterned fabric
- Small tacks
- Fine sandpaper or sanding block
- Tack cloth
- Paintbrushes
- Sharp scissors
- Hot-glue gun and glue sticks
- Hammer

INSTRUCTIONS

1. Remove any pulls or handles from the cupboard and set them aside. (Or save them for another purpose and make your own pulls like the ones shown here; we tell you how in step 8.)

2. Lightly sand the cupboard. Wipe the sanding dust from the cabinet with the tack cloth.

3. Pour a small amount of acrylic paint into the plastic container. Thin the paint with water, using a bit of water at a time. Brush the thinned paint onto the back side of the cupboard to test the color. Add more water if necessary; you want a thinned color wash that allows the grain of the wood to show through.

4. When you're happy with your paint consistency, brush the paint onto the cupboard. Let it dry. If you like, lightly sand the surface of the cupboard and remove a bit of color. Or, you might want to give the cupboard an additional coat of paint to intensify the color. Let it dry, then lightly sand the surface.

5. Cut the flowers from the paper. Bold, simple shapes are easiest to cut out and apply.

6. Apply a thin coat of the acrylic medium or thinned white craft glue to the back of a flower. Place the flower on the cupboard, smoothing out any wrinkles with your fingers. Apply additional flowers until you have the coverage you want. Let them dry.

7. If you like, paint the cupboard with a thin coat of polyurethane.

8. For handle pulls like the ones shown here, paint the wooden craft beads and let them dry. Cut two strips from the patterned fabric, each approximately 3 x 6 inches (7.6 x 15.2 cm). Roll a strip to create a long, narrow roll. Hot glue the long edge of the fabric. Run a bead of hot glue into the hole in one of the wooden beads, and insert one end of the roll into the bead. Let the glue cool. Use additional glue to secure the roll in the bead, if necessary. Thread the roll into the hole in the cupboard (left by the removed handle) and tug it through until the craft bead hangs down approximately 2 inches (5.1 cm). Trim the length of the roll on the back side of the cupboard door to about ½ inch (1.3 cm). Secure the roll by hammering in a small tack. Repeat to create the second handle.

MATERIALS & TOOLS

NOTE: The measurements provided here are approximations. The size of your mirror should dictate the length of your dowel and the size of your wooden base.

- Wooden circular base, 6 to 8 inches (15.2 to 20.3 cm) in diameter
- Round mirror, approximately 3 to 6 inches (7.6 to 15.2 cm) in diameter
- Heavy cardboard box (Recycle a shipping box or milk box from the grocery store.)
- Small tacks
- ½ inch (1.3 cm) wooden dowel, 12 to 16 inches (30.5 to 40.6 cm) long
- Wood glue
- Wallpaper paste
- Container for paste; a small plastic bowl works well
- Torn newspaper strips, about 1 inch (2.5 cm) wide
- Gesso
- Acrylic paints
- Drill and drill bits
- Pencil
- Craft knife
- Small paintbrush
- Hot-glue gun and glue sticks

INSTRUCTIONS

1. Drill a hole in the center of your wooden base equal to the diameter of your dowel. Set it aside.

2. Trace your round mirror on the cardboard with a pencil. Draw five or more petals around the mirror. Cut out the flower shape with a craft knife.

3. Use the small tacks to secure the flower shape to the dowel.

4. Draw a leaf shape on cardboard, and cut it out. Tack it to the dowel.

5. Use wood glue to secure the dowel in the hole you drilled in the base. Let it dry.

6. Mix the wallpaper paste according to the manufacturer's instructions.

7. Dip the newspaper strips, one at a time, into the paste. Cover the dowel, base, leaf, and petals with a single layer of coated newspaper strips. Let the piece dry.

8. Cover the flower with at least three layers of coated newspaper strips. Allow each layer to dry before applying another layer.

9. Paint the entire assembly with a coat of gesso. Allow it to dry. If the newsprint still peeks through, paint additional coats of gesso on the surface.

10. Paint the stem, base, and leaf of the flower green. Modulate the color with lighter shades of green, if you like.

11. You can paint the petals a solid color or replicate the patterned petals we've painted here. If you're using more than one color, let each color dry before you apply the next.

12. Hot glue the mirror into the center of the flower shape.

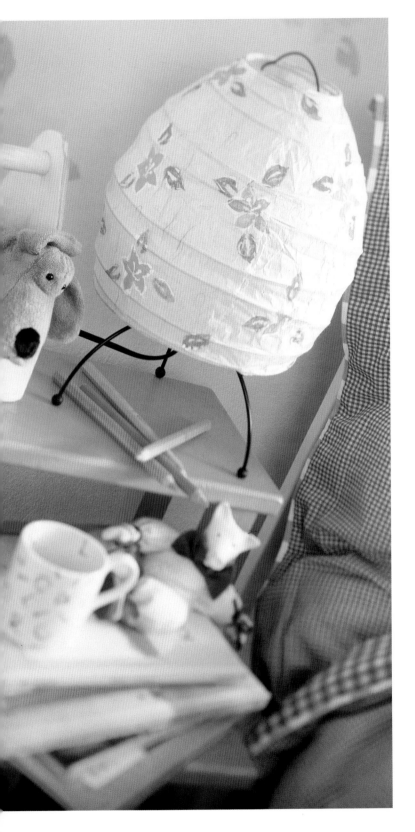

MATERIALS & TOOLS

- Tissue paper featuring a floral motif
- Lamp with a ribbed rice-paper shade
- Plastic trash bag
- Newspaper
- Acrylic medium or white craft glue lightly thinned with water
- Sharp scissors
- Small paintbrush

INSTRUCTIONS

1. Cut out the tissue-paper flowers, leaving a border, then trim them more closely. Set them aside and out of the way of curious little fingers and drafts that might set them aflutter.

2. To give the lampshade extra support, fit a plastic trash bag inside the shade and stuff it with wadded newspaper balls. When your shade can stand unsupported and with as flat a surface as possible, proceed to the next step.

3. Apply a thin coat of acrylic medium or thinned white glue to the back side of a flower. Carefully lift the flower and place it on the shade. Smooth the flower with your fingers and remove any wrinkles that appear. Rotate the shade and place another flower on the surface. Keep rotating the shade and adding flowers until the shade is covered to your satisfaction. Let the flowers dry.

4. Brush a light coat of acrylic medium or thinned craft glue on the flowers. Be careful not to brush the medium too far beyond the flower edges; you simply want to seal them in place. Let the flowers dry.

5. Remove the wadded newspaper and the trash bag. Hang the shade on the lamp.

5 OCEAN VIEW

Maybe it's all the daydreaming on the part of their sun-deprived parents that starts kids thinking about sandy beaches and breaking waves. Or, perhaps it's their own happy memories of building sandcastles and collecting shells. Whichever, a whole lot of kids love the idea of turning their rooms into one long summer vacation by the sea.

weathered wood

Without regular doses of salty air, beating sun, and strong gusts blowing in off the water, the wood in your child's room is in danger of looking as good as new for a very long time. Fortunately, there are a number of simple decorative painting techniques that'll give shutters, furniture, and wooden trim the exposed-to-the-elements look a proper seaside retreat needs.

WEATHERED WOOD *step-by-step*

MATERIALS & TOOLS

- Latex paint in both a light and dark shade of the color you're working with
- Water
- Bucket (for mixing paint with water)
- Stir stick
- Paintbrush
- Clean rags
- Sandpaper, 120 grit or finer

INSTRUCTIONS

For best results use these painting techniques on unfinished wood that is free of all dirt and grime. First, paint on a base coat of your lighter color, and let it dry completely. Then use one of the following approaches.

■ Mix the darker shade of paint with water and stir well. You'll need to experiment with the ratio of water to paint. For a very thin color wash, use more water. Paint a wash of the darker color over the entire surface of the wood. Allow the paint to sit for a few minutes, then wipe some of the paint away with a clean rag to give it an uneven or weathered appearance. For more color, give the piece a second wash.

■ Apply the darker paint to a paintbrush. Offload the brush onto a rag until it's almost dry. Paint the piece with the almost-dry brush, dragging the tip of the brush in long strokes until the piece is entirely covered. Apply several almost-dry coats in this fashion, building up the layers of top color.

■ Paint the entire piece with the darker paint. Allow the paint to dry thoroughly. Use fine-grit sandpaper to lightly sand away some of the darker color to reveal the lighter shade underneath. Sand very lightly to prevent exposing the raw wood.

pickling

Pickling is another surface decoration technique for wood. Use it when you want a floor or furniture piece to display a satisfyingly sun-bleached look atop visible wood grain.

MATERIALS & TOOLS

- Flat white latex paint
- Furniture wax (optional)
- Varnish (optional)
- Medium steel wool or wire brush
- Clean rags
- Old paintbrush
- Fine-grit sandpaper
- Tack cloth

INSTRUCTIONS

Pickling works best on open-grained wood that is free of paint, varnish, or polish.

1. Using steel wool or a wire brush, open up the grain of the wood by brushing firmly in the direction of the grain. Wipe away all dust and residue with a clean rag.

2. Use an old paintbrush to work the latex paint deep into the grain of the wood. Wipe away the excess paint with a clean rag, leaving the paint in the grain and crevices of the wood. Work small areas at a time; the paint dries quickly. Once you've worked the entire surface, allow the paint to dry thoroughly.

3. Lightly sand the entire surface. Remove all residue with a tack or lint-free cloth.

4. For a more natural look, rub furniture wax onto the surface, then buff the piece. For a more durable finish (on a floor, for example), apply several coats of varnish, lightly sanding in between coats.

painted sand pails

Suspend them up high for adults-only storage, or scatter them about so everyone can use them to tote Legos and puzzle pieces from one end of the room to the other. The metal buckets are an inexpensive paint-store buy, and the simple shapes make this an easy project for kids and parents to tackle together.

MATERIALS & TOOLS

- Metal paint buckets (You'll find them in the paint section of your local home improvement or paint store.)
- Small paintbrushes
- Acrylic paints in blue, white, and two shades of orange

INSTRUCTIONS

1. Paint large fish and starfish shapes with the orange paints around the sides of one bucket. Let the paint dry, then re-coat the shapes if necessary.

2. Between each fish, paint a small blue heart. Let the paint dry,

3. Use the white paint and your smallest paintbrush to add smiling faces and scales on the fish and other details that capture your fancy. If you wish, turn a fish into a whale with the addition of a blue spout of water.

4. Beach cabanas adorn the other bucket. Paint white house shapes around the bucket. Let them dry. Add the details—roof, door, windows—with blue paint. Let them dry.

5. Paint a small seashell between each cabana using orange paint. Let it dry, then add details to the shell with the blue paint.

fossil wall plaques

Here's an inventive piece of wall art that's perfect for a marine biologist in the making—or for kids who simply love collecting specimens. You can make a bold statement with all nine panels, or scale the project down to just a few if that better suits your room size.

MATERIALS & TOOLS

- Fossil patterns, page 124
- Low-tack painter's tape, about ½ inch (1.3 cm) wide
- Acrylic paints in nine colors. (We've used gray blue, olive green, pastel blue, lilac, sea blue, aubergine, taupe, gray, and sand. Feel free to choose another combination that better matches your room.)
- Newspapers
- 9 squares of .080 (or thicker) clear acrylic sheeting, each 20 inches (50.8 cm) square
- Transparent acrylic varnish/medium
- Clear, white, or crystal glitter
- Length of utility link chain, 18 links. (Each link should measure approximately ½ x 1 inch [1.3 x 2.5 cm].)
- Six #8 plastic wall anchors
- Six #8 screw eyes
- Tape measure or ruler
- Pencil
- Paintbrushes
- Drill and drill bits
- Heavy-duty wire cutters or hacksaw
- Pliers

INSTRUCTIONS

1. Measure and mark a large square on the wall 60 x 60 inches (153 x 153 cm). Mark the top, bottom, and sides of the square at 20 and 40 inches (50.8 and 101.6 cm). Lightly connect the marks to divide the large square into nine squares.

2. Mask off each of the horizontal lines with painter's tape. Align the tape above the top line and under the remaining three lines.

3. Mask off the vertical lines with the painter's tape. Align the tape to the left of the left-hand line; align the tape to the right of the remaining lines.

4. Paint each square a different color. Let the paint dry. Give each square a second coat, if necessary. Remove the tape when the paint is dry.

5. Enlarge the patterns on page 124 so the shapes fit comfortably in your squares.

6. Spread a layer of newspaper down on a table.

7. Lay a square of acrylic sheeting over a pattern. Use a small paintbrush to paint the shape on the acrylic sheeting with the transparent varnish, then sprinkle it with a thin coat of the glass glitter. Let it dry.

8. Pour the excess glitter off into a container. Touch up any areas that were not coated well with varnish. Re-coat the piece with glitter.

9. Repeat steps 6 through 8 for each acrylic sheeting panel.

10. Drill two holes at the top of each panel. Mark the points for the holes 2 inches (5.1 cm) in from each side and ¼ inch (6 mm) down from the top. Mark and drill holes at the bottom of six panels, using the same measurements.

11. Cut the chain links with a wire cutter or hacksaw. Use the pliers to open them slightly. Slip them into the drilled holes.

12. Align the top of one panel with the top and side painted edges of a square. Mark the top points of the links on the wall. These marks are where you'll need to drill holes for the plastic wall anchors. Drill a hole at each marked point, using an appropriately sized drill bit.

13. Insert the wall anchors into the holes and screw in the screw eyes. Hang the links on the screw eyes and check the alignment.

14. Hang a second panel underneath the first with two links. Use the pliers to adjust the links if the alignment is not to your liking. Repeat for the third panel.

15. Repeat steps 12 through 14 for each column of panels.

cabana cover

This stylish coverup lets a standard shelving unit go through life disguised as a bathhouse. You can still use the shelves to store all sorts of ordinary items. It's just that now they'll be attractively concealed behind the cover's tie-back flaps.

CABANA COVER *step-by-step*

MATERIALS & TOOLS

- Two triangles cut from plywood (The base of the triangles should match the width of your shelving unit.)
- 4 corner irons and screws for attaching
- 1 dowel rod as long as the depth of your shelving unit
- Flat bed sheet (Determine the size you need based on the height, depth, and width of your shelving unit.)
- Mercerized cotton thread
- Thumbtacks
- 2 large grommets
- 4 yards (3.6 m) cording
- 4 large wooden balls with holes running through them (Craft stores carry these.)
- 4 stuffed fish or other decorative accents
- Standard measuring and marking tools
- Electric drill and appropriate-size bits to drill holes for the dowel rod and to predrill holes for the corner-iron screws
- Screwdriver
- Scissors
- Iron
- Sewing machine
- Straight pins
- Grommet maker

INSTRUCTIONS

1. Predrill holes, then screw the corner irons to the backs of the plywood triangles (two per triangle), approximately 6 inches (15.2 cm) in from the outer corners.

2. Drill a hole close to the top corner peak of the back of each triangle, so you can insert a dowel rod to stabilize the two triangles in the next step (see figure 1).

3. Place one triangle at the front edge of the top of the shelving unit, positioning it so the front of the triangle is flush with the front of the unit and matching the corners. The hole you drilled in step 2 should be on the back side. Make pencil marks where you need to predrill holes for screwing the corner irons into the shelving unit, then drill the holes and screw the corner irons to the unit. Repeat the process to screw the other triangle to the back edge of the top of the unit. Insert the dowel rod into the holes you drilled in step 2, trimming it to fit if necessary.

4. Lay out your sheet. You want the wide hem (the end typically at the top on a bed) to be your Cabana Cover's finished bottom hem. The length from this hem up to the other end (which will hang at the Cabana's top) should match the height of your shelving unit plus the measurement of the angle side of your triangles (see figure 2). Cut off excess fabric (if necessary) from the end opposite the wide hem.

5. Fold back 2½ inches (6.4 cm) on both of the Cabana Cover's side edges, press the folds, fold inside the folded area again, and press and stitch to create 1¼-inch (3.2 cm) finished hems.

6. Wrap the sheet around the shelving unit, wrong side of the sheet facing out. Match the center backs of the sheet and the unit. Bring the ends around to the front, adjust the overlap (this should be about 4 inches [10.2 cm]), thumbtack the sheet in place at the front and back peak points, and mark the center front.

7. Bring the portions of the sheet covering the unit's two sides up to the center of the dowel rod, and pin them together using a ½ inch (1.3 cm) seam. The two sides now form the top of the roof; the front and back are hanging loosely at this point (see figure 3).

8. Starting with the back section first, pin the angled sides together along the edge of the triangle, from the top point down to the side corners (see figure 4). Repeat this process on the front triangle, which will be slightly trickier because of the overlapping fabric.

9. Remove the pinned cover, take it to the sewing machine, and stitch the angles, removing pins as you go. Start by stitching the top seam (its end points are at the tops of the two triangles). Next, stitch both sides of the back triangle, starting at the top seam and stitching to the corners. Repeat the process for the front triangle. Trim the excess fabric to within ½ inch (1.3 cm) of the seam.

10. Place the stitched sheet on the peaked shelving unit, right side out, and check the fit. Mark a place for a grommet at each side corner, approximately 36 inches (91.4 cm) up from the floor. Using the grommet tool, place grommets at the marks.

11. Cut the cording in half, double each half, and insert each half through one of the grommets. Slide the wooden balls and other decorative accents to the ends of the cords. Loop one end of the cord into the other on each side to hold the Cabana Cover flaps back.

12. If you like, sew a fabric heart or other symbol to the top of the cover's overlap to help hold the flaps in place. Sew the symbol from the back side, tacking the two flaps together when you do.

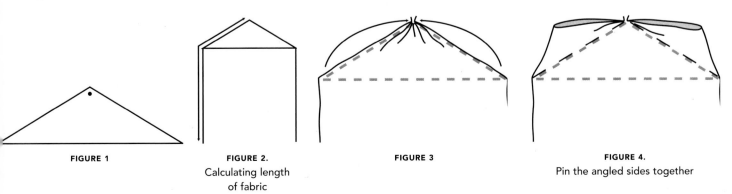

FIGURE 1

FIGURE 2.
Calculating length
of fabric

FIGURE 3

FIGURE 4.
Pin the angled sides together

maritime stripes

What a relief to know how simple it can be to carry out a grand plan. If you want to conjure up images of sailors and seagoing vessels without a huge amount of work, some bold swashes of alternating navy and white on a wall will do the trick.

MATERIALS & TOOLS

- Flat latex paint in white and navy
- String (for technique #1)
- Adhesive putty
- Paint roller (Long-pile rollers are fluffy and produce a wobbly, uneven edge. A sponge roller creates a neater, straight edge. If you don't plan to tape off the walls, choose your roller type according to the results you want.)
- Paint tray
- Low-tack painter's tape
- Measuring tape or straightedge ruler
- Pencil
- Scissors
- 4-foot (1.2 m) level (for technique #2)
- Small detail brush (for technique #2)

INSTRUCTIONS

1. Paint your wall white.

2. Mask off the molding at the top and bottom of the wall, using painter's tape.

3. Measure the width of the wall. Decide on the width of your stripes, so you can create an equal number of them. (It's best to do the math and map out your design before you begin marking your walls.) Divide the width of the wall in half. Start measuring your spaces from the middle of the wall. Center the width of your first stripe and work outward to each side. Use a pencil to mark out your intervals. Then, use one of the two following techniques to paint your stripes.

Technique #1

To create a more hand-painted look where the edges aren't perfectly straight, as we have here, use the width of your roller as the width of your stripe.

1. Cut several lengths of string to the height of the wall. Use adhesive putty to stick the string to the top of the wall at the proper distance from the center point.

2. To keep the string straight as it hangs, wrap the end of the string in adhesive putty to create a plumb line. (You can also use a thumbtack to attach the string to the top of the wall and tie a washer to the bottom of string to create the plumb line.)

3. Attach lengths of string at all the measured intervals to mark your stripes. Using the strings as your guide for aligning the stripes, load the navy paint onto a dampened roller and roll the stripe onto the wall. Skip every other set of strings to create the alternate white spaces (stripes). It may help to put a small "X" mark in pencil in the spaces that you will paint navy.

Technique #2

For cleaner edges, here's another approach.

1. Use a level to pencil in very thin parallel guidelines (based on the intervals you marked) for taping. Mask off these lines, using low-tack painter's tape, to create stripes of the proper width. Apply your tape inside the white spaces (see figure 1).

2. Use the roller to paint navy stripes between the taped spaces. Gently pull off the tape before the paint begins to dry.

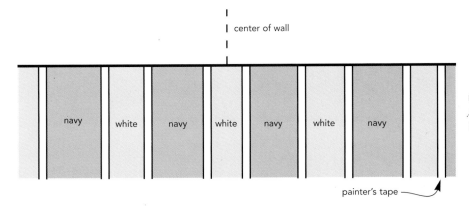

center of wall

navy   white   navy   white   navy   white   navy

painter's tape

FIGURE 1.
Apply the painter's tape inside the white spaces.

fish market

It's absolutely unavoidable. Toys, scattered across every available surface, will be a major component of your child's room "decor" for about a decade or so. Make sure a few of them are stuffed fabric sea creatures that support the rest of the room's nautical look, and it will appear as though there's a bit of method to the madness.

MATERIALS & TOOLS

- Fish Market patterns, page 125
- Variety of leftover fabrics in different patterns and colors, cut in 6 x 8-inch (15.2 x 20.3 cm) pieces
- Embroidery floss in contrasting colors
- Mercerized cotton thread in coordinating colors
- Polyester stuffing
- Chalk pencil or water soluble marking pen
- Large-eyed needle
- Straight pins
- Sewing machine
- Standard measuring and marking tools
- Scissors
- Small pointed dowel or pencil
- Regular sewing needle

Note: When you're embroidering the features on your sea creatures, always use three strands of embroidery floss.

INSTRUCTIONS

1. Using the patterns on page 125 and a chalk pencil or water soluble marking pen, trace the sea creatures you want to make onto the wrong sides of your fabric pieces. Do not cut your pieces out at this point.

2. FOR THE OCTOPUS: use embroidery floss to stitch an "X" for each eye on the front of the fabric. Pin together the front piece and another fabric piece, which will become the back. Using your machine's smallest stitch, stitch along the transferred pattern line, carefully pivoting at inner curves and leaving an opening at least 1½ inches (3.8 cm) wide at the center top of the head. Trim away the outside fabric to within ¼ inch (6 mm) of your stitching line. Carefully clip the points of the legs just to the stitching line, and clip all the curves. Turn the piece. Use the dowel or the eraser end of the pencil to push small bits of stuffing into the ends of the legs. Continue stuffing the rest of the octopus, then slipstitch the opening closed, using a regular sewing needle and thread.

3. FOR THE CRAB: use embroidery floss and a satin stitch (see figure 1) to create the eyes. Follow the instructions in step 2 for sewing, turning, and stuffing the body. Create the claws by tracing two pieces per claw, sewing the sides (right sides together), and leaving the ends open for turning and stuffing. Clip the seams, then turn and stuff the claws. Fold back a scant ¼ inch (6 mm) of raw edge at the openings, pin the claws in place, and hand-stitch them onto the body, using a blanket stitch (see figure 2).

4. FOR THE FISH: cut out the shapes, with an additional ¼-inch (6 mm) seam all around. On the bottom half, create scales with embroidery floss by making single stitches. Add eyes to the head piece by cutting small scraps of white fabric, folding all the edges under, hand-sewing them in place, then using embroidery floss to stitch "X" shapes for the eyes. On one head section, fold back ¼ inch (6 mm) of the end (where it attaches to the tail section), and sew it to one tail section, using a zigzag stitch. Repeat the process for the other head and tail sections (so you've got front and back pieces). Pin the front and back pieces together, right sides together, and stitch them, leaving an opening at the bottom edge. Clip the curves, being careful not to cut through the stitches, turn the piece, stuff it, and slipstitch the opening closed.

5. FOR THE BUOY: follow the same process described for making the fish with a couple of adjustments. Instead of scales, embroider wavy lines. And instead of "X" shapes on the white patches for eyes, embroider (or draw on) numbers.

FIGURE 1. Satin stitch

FIGURE 2. Blanket stitch

COLOR
THEIR
WORLD

Soon enough in life they'll receive plenty of signals that it's best to tone down their palettes. They'll hear that drab-colored suits are the sensible choice. And red cars only attract the attention of traffic cops. But for now, give them an early and healthy grounding in the virtues of purple walls, floors covered with orange flowers, and blue-and-green polka dots everywhere.

two-tone light cover

Start with two vivid shades created from the sort of sturdy material used to make knapsacks and good-quality kites. Form it around lengths of wire, and you've got a bright light cover that casts a colorful glow.

TWO-TONE LIGHT COVER
step-by-step

MATERIALS & TOOLS

- 2 colors of ripstop nylon, each ½ yard (.45 m) long
- 14-gauge wire
- Matching sewing thread
- Fine-gauge wire (22-gauge or smaller)
- 4 tassels
- Scissors
- Ruler
- Wire cutters
- Sewing machine or fabric glue
- Heavy duty needle-nose pliers
- Pliers
- Tapestry needle

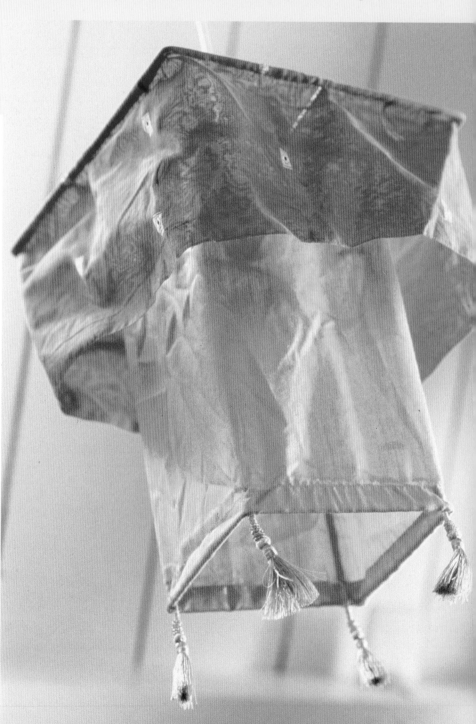

INSTRUCTIONS

This shade is designed to hang over an existing pendant fixture with the globe removed. But with a bit of ingenuity, you can adapt the instructions to make a cover for any sort of ceiling fixture.

1. Measure and cut one color of the ripstop nylon to make a 10 x 48-inch (25.4 cm x 1.2 m) rectangle.

2. Measure and cut the second color of ripstop to make an 18 x 32-inch (45.7 x 81.2 cm) rectangle.

3. Measure and use the wire cutters to cut the 14-gauge wire into two lengths measuring 48 and 32 inches (1.2 m and 81.2 cm) each. Set them aside.

4. Create a ¾-inch (1.9 cm) casing in one long side of each piece of ripstop. All you need to do is fold over ¾ inch (1.9 cm) of fabric along the edge, then sew it or use a line of fabric glue near the raw edge of the fabric. If you use glue, let it dry completely.

5. Use the needle-nose pliers to create a small hook approximately ³⁄₁₆ inch long (4.8 mm) at each end of both lengths of wire.

6. Thread a wire length through each casing (longer wire through the longer casing, shorter wire through the shorter one).

7. Create a roughly square shape for each shade. Use the pliers to make a right-angle bend in the encased wire at the halfway point of each length of fabric. Then make two additional bends to create a square, bringing the hook ends together. You may need to "scrunch" up the fabric to join the hooks. When you are happy with the shapes, use the pliers to close the hooks tightly together. Set both shades to the side.

8. Measure and cut two lengths of fine-gauge wire, each approximately 36 inches (91 cm) in length. Thread one length through the eye of the tapestry needle, and make a bend in the end approximately 1 inch (2.5 cm) from the end of the wire. This bend will act as a knot and prevent you from pulling the wire completely through the fabric.

9. You are going to make the hanger for the shade. The hanger is created by two pairs of parallel wires forming a cross. Lay the larger shade, wire side down, on a flat surface. Place the smaller shade inside the larger one.

10. Center the needle on an inside edge of the large shade, against the wire, and bring it to the outside. Bring the needle around the frame wire and pass it back through to the outside to lock it on. Bring the needle down ½ inch (1.3 cm) and back through the fabric. Bring the needle around the frame wire again and pass it through to the inside (see figure 1). This will secure the thin wire.

11. Bring the threaded needle through the smaller shade to its opposite side. Continue to bring the needle through to the opposite side of the larger shade. Bring the needle out and back in, locking on the wire, as you did in step 10, then bringing it up ½ inch (1.3 cm), and locking on again. Pass the needle back across to the tail you left at the start (see figure 2). Twist the wire ends together, making the wire taut without tearing the fabric.

12. Repeat steps 10 and 11 on the other sides of the shades to create another set of parallel wires that form a cross shape with the first two (see figure 3).

13. Sew premade tassels to the shade where you want them.

14. Spread the hanger wires in the square they form in the center of the shades, and hang the shade on the fixture. You will need to twist the wires to secure the shade on the fixture. Be sure the hanger wires are not touching any exposed electrical wire.

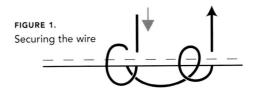

FIGURE 1.
Securing the wire

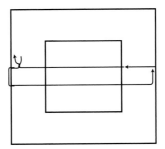

FIGURE 2.

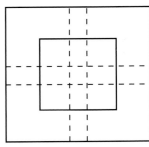

FIGURE 3.

forever plaid

What a charming surprise when this pattern we associate with scarves or skirts turns up on a piece of painted furniture. Brushing on a not-so-traditional tartan design is an original way to add accent color to a room.

FOREVER PLAID *step-by-step*

MATERIALS & TOOLS

- Primer
- White latex paint, eggshell finish
- Colored latex paint
- Varnish
- Screwdriver
- Sandpaper
- Paintbrushes
- Framing square, triangle or ruler
- Pencil
- Low-tack painter's tape, 2 inches (5.1 cm) wide
- Foam roller or seam roller, 2 x 1 inches (5.1 x 2.5 cm)
- Pan or dish to hold paint
- Clean rags

INSTRUCTIONS

1. Remove all the hardware from the drawers. Sand and prime the chest, and paint it with two coats of white paint.

2. Use painter's tape to mask off the outer edges of the chest, where you want it to remain white.

3. To create vertical stripes, start in the top center of chest, and use the framing square and a pencil to measure out and mark equidistant intervals across the face of the chest. The width of the painter's tape dictates the width of your stripes. For example, if your chest is 26 inches (66 cm) wide, you'll make your first pencil mark directly in the center of the chest, at 13 inches (33 cm). Center a strip of painter's tape over the middle pencil line. Then, measure and mark 2-inch (5.1 cm) intervals on each side of the centered tape.

4. Use painter's tape to mask off every other 2-inch (5.1 cm) interval (these masked-off areas will remain white). Tape over the drawers and down to the base of the chest, pressing the tape down firmly as you go, and keeping the tape lines parallel.

5. When all vertical tape is in place, roll on the colored paint between all the taped areas.

6. When you're finished, gently pull off the strips of tape before the paint begins to dry. Allow the paint to dry thoroughly (at least 2 hours).

7. Mark and mask horizontal spacing the same way you marked and masked the vertical spacing, starting at the middle of the side of the chest.

8. Paint colored horizontal stripes with the roller. Remove the tape and allow the paint to dry.

9. If you want to paint the sides of the chest, repeat the same process on each side.

10. Apply several coats of varnish to protect the surface, sanding lightly in between coats, then secure the hardware back onto the chest.

curtains in three-way color

Forget fussy ruffles and elaborate designs. Using fabric simply is the current trend in window treatments. (About time, say busy parents decorating on tight time schedules.) What could be simpler than starting with the bed-sheet pattern you're already using in the room and playing it out in three complementary colors?

CLIPPED CURTAINS *step-by-step*

MATERIALS & TOOLS

- Three (or more; see step 1) twin-size flat sheets in coordinating colors/patterns
- All-purpose mercerized cotton thread in coordinating colors
- Curtain rings and clips
- Standard measuring and marking tools
- Iron
- Sewing machine

INSTRUCTIONS

1. Determine exactly how many sheets you need based on the width of your window. You want your curtains to have double or triple fullness. A standard twin sheet is typically 66 inches (167.6 cm) wide. If you're working with a window that is also that wide, you'll need three sheets for triple fullness.

2. Measure the height of your window. If it's less than 96 inches (2.4 m) (the standard length of a twin sheet), cut off the excess, fold the edge over 2 inches (5.1 cm), press it, fold the folded area in half again, and stitch close to the fold to create a hem.

3. Use the sheet's existing wide hem as the top of your curtain. Hang it using evenly spaced clips attached to rings that slip onto the curtain rod.

4. There's no need to sew the sheets together, but you can if you like. If you do, you can achieve a nice look by also sewing buttons randomly along the long edges where the sheets are stitched together. Using different sizes and colors of buttons adds even more interest.

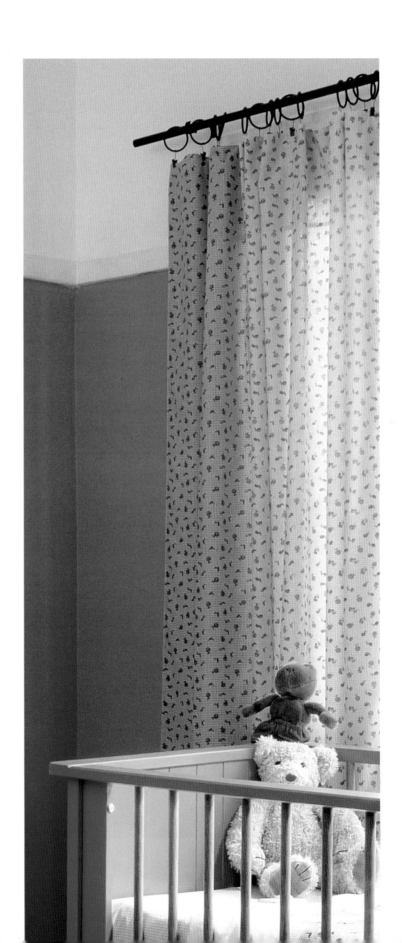

MATERIALS & TOOLS

- 1 twin sheet or pillowcase (or excess sheet fabric from the Clipped Curtain project)
- All-purpose mercerized cotton thread in coordinating colors
- Small wooden dowels
- Small cup hooks or eye hooks (4 per door)
- Standard measuring and marking tools
- Scissors
- Sewing machine

INSTRUCTIONS

1. Measure the opening of the cupboard door you want to cover, then cut a piece of sheet fabric two to three times as wide as the opening and about 4 inches (10.2 cm) higher. For example, if the opening is 10 inches wide by 8 inches high (25.4 x 20.3 cm), cut a piece of fabric 24 to 32 inches wide (61 to 81.3 cm) and 12 inches (30.5 cm) high.

2. Create 1-inch (2.5 cm) hems on the two sides of the fabric by folding the fabric over and stitching close to the folded edges.

3. On the edges that will be the top and bottom of the curtains, measure and press a 1-inch (2.5 cm) hem. Fold under the raw edge ¼ inch (6 mm), and stitch close to that folded edge. This creates a casing for inserting the dowel rod.

4. Cut the two small dowel rods to lengths that match the width of your cupboard door openings plus 1 inch (2.5 cm). Insert the rods into the casings.

5. Affix the cup hooks or eye hooks inside the cupboard around the door frame, at least 1 inch (2.5 cm) above and below the corners. Fit the dowels into the hooks, making sure the fabric is pulled taut. Arrange the gathers to fit.

circles & stripes

If your kids spoke the language of interior designers, they'd talk to you about the importance of movement, design detail, and combined color tones. All they'd really be saying, of course, is that it sure would be fun to have a bunch of colorful circles and stripes jazzing up their walls and floors.

MATERIALS & TOOLS

- Pale blue latex flat or satin finish paint (walls)
- Kraft paper
- Latex paint in medium blue and several other intermediate shades of blue (one slightly darker for the striped rug and another for the floor), green, and white
- Blank stencil film (or clear acetate)
- Small dishes, lids, or other round objects to use as templates
- Dense-cell foam (Blank foam sheets are available at craft stores.)
- Wooden blocks
- Contact cement
- Spray adhesive
- Varnish
- Foam rollers (You'll need regular rollers for the walls, ceiling, and floor, and various-sized rollers for details, including stencil and foam rollers in various widths.)
- Paintbrush (optional)
- Straightedge ruler
- Pencil
- Level
- Low-tack painter's tape
- Paint pad (optional)
- Scissors
- Detail brush (for cleaning up errors)
- Small, round, foam stencil brush with wooden handle
- Craft knife
- Self-healing cutting mat
- Sandpaper
- Clean rags and/or tack cloth

INSTRUCTIONS

Begin by painting the ceiling pale blue or white and the walls pale blue. Let all the paint dry thoroughly.

Ceiling

1. Use the straightedge to measure down from the ceiling the width of your border. Mark this distance lightly with a pencil around the entire room. Use a level to connect the pencil marks evenly. Use low-tack painter's tape to mask off the line around the entire room. This border will extend up onto the ceiling.

2. Use a roller to paint the border inside the masked line. Use the paint pad, if you like, for the corners and around the ceiling line.

3. To extend the border design onto the ceiling with a curved line, as we have here, begin by laying several feet of kraft paper onto a work surface. Use a pencil to create a large, sweeping curved line on the paper. Cut out the curve carefully with the scissors. Use painter's tape on the straight side of the paper to hold the paper on the ceiling. Lightly tack down the curved side with tape. Tape the paper template around the entire border of the ceiling. Hold down the curved edge of the paper as you roll the paint on with a small roller, cutting the paint into the curve. When the paint is dry, pull the template down and use the small roller to fill in the remainder of the space between the curve and the wall. Touch up any mistakes with a small detail brush. Allow the paint to dry before painting your wall designs.

Wall Stripes

1. Measure the width of the wall and decide on the width of your stripes. Starting in the center of the wall, use the straightedge and pencil to mark off the intervals for your stripes. Use the level to draw very light parallel pencil lines to act as guides for masking off the stripes.

2. Mask off these lines, using low-tack painter's tape, to create stripes of the proper width. Apply your tape inside the pale-blue spaces (see figure 1).

3. Use the roller to paint medium-blue stripes between the taped spaces. (You may want to mark a small "X" on the stripes you'll be painting to avoid confusion.)

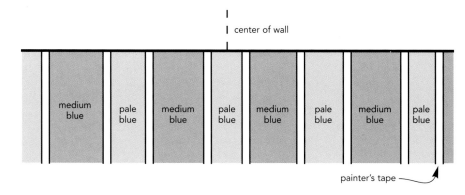

center of wall

| medium blue | pale blue | medium blue | pale blue | medium blue | pale blue | medium blue | pale blue |

painter's tape

FIGURE 1.
Apply the painter's tape inside the pale blue spaces.

4. When the blue stripes have dried thoroughly, use tape to mask off lines just inside each side of the blue stripes. Decide on the width of your thin white stripes. Measure over this distance on each side of the blue stripes, and once again tape off parallel lines.

5. Use a small roller to paint between the masked-off areas.

6. Allow these stripes to dry, then use the small, round, foam stencil brush to make a dotted design alongside the stripes. Practice using the brush on paper before applying the dots to the wall.

Wall Circles

1. Lay your blank stencil film on the cutting mat. Choose a round object that matches the size you want your widest circle. Lay the object on the blank stencil, and use a craft knife to carefully cut around it to create the circle stencil.

2. Choose two progressively smaller circular objects to use as templates for the interior circles. You'll make stamps for these. Trace around the first object onto the blank foam sheet. Use scissors to cut out this circle. Repeat this process for the smallest circle stamp.

3. Use contact cement to mount each cut stamp to a wooden block.

4. Decide on the overall placement of your circles, then begin with the large stencil circle. Use the spray adhesive to hold the stencil in place on the wall. Use a stencil roller to apply white paint. Off-load the roller onto paper so that it is almost dry before painting the stencil. It's less likely paint will seep under the stencil and blur the design if the roller isn't heavily loaded with paint. Reposition the stencil all around the wall to create your overall pattern. Let the paint dry thoroughly.

5. Use the circle block stamps to fill in the next color. Use green, medium blue, or light blue alternately to create these designs. Apply paint to the stamp using a small foam roller. Practice on paper first to adjust the pressure needed to create a clean print. Stamp the designs inside the white circles, cleaning the stamp thoroughly between colors. When all the paint is dry, repeat this process using the smaller block stamp.

6. Use the small, round, foam stencil brush to paint the center dots.

Striped Floor Rug

1. Prep the entire floor for painting by sanding lightly and removing residue with a tack cloth.

2. Roll or brush blue paint onto the entire floor. Allow the paint to dry.

3. Use a straightedge and level to pencil in the outline of the painted rug. Tape off the border with low-tack painter's tape.

4. Decide on the width of the stripes. (The rug we've created here has very wide blue stripes and narrower green stripes.) Measure again and mark off the intervals. Tape off for the blue stripes first. Lay the tape down outside the lines for the blue stripes. Use a roller to fill in between the taped lines. When the blue paint dries, gently peel the tape away.

5. Tape inside the blue stripe to mask off the area for the green stripes. Paint the green stripes using a roller.

6. Apply several coats of clear varnish to seal the floor, sanding lightly in between coats.

sleeping
tent

This dreamy little number can be used first as a crib or playpen cover and later as a canopy for a twin bed or a suspended tent in the center of the room. Use shimmery, sheer material in an exotic color to inspire naptime adventures in far-off lands.

MATERIALS & TOOLS

- Gauze-type fabric, 54 inches (137.2 cm) wide (You need 1 yard [.9 m] per foot [.3 m] of floor-to-ceiling height.)
- Mercerized thread in colors that match your fabrics
- 1 package bias hem facing tape, 1⅞ inches wide (4.8 cm) (Packages typically contain 2½ yards [2.2 m].)
- 1 yard (.9 m) of heavier-weight fabric, 54 inches (137.2 cm) wide, in a contrasting or coordinating color
- 6 feet (1.8 m) of #4 solid bare copper wire (Home improvement stores sell this in their electrical sections; it's used to ground panel boxes.)
- 1 yard (.9 m) small cord or string
- Sturdy ceiling hook
- Standard measuring and marking tools
- Sharpened dowel
- Scissors
- Iron
- Sewing machine
- Straight pins
- Bodkin (a tweezer-like tool you'll use to insert the cord in its casing)
- Pliers
- Strong tape (Electrical tape works well.)

INSTRUCTIONS

Gauze Panels and Tent Top

1. Cut three sections of gauze, each 1 foot (.3 m) shorter than your floor-to-ceiling height. Press under a scant ½-inch (1.3 cm) hem on all the bottom edges, and stitch the hems. You can leave the finished selvage edges of the pieces as they are.

2. Overlap the side edges of the three pieces by 6 to 8 inches (15.2 to 20.3 cm) at the top, and pin the overlaps, forming a circle with the fabric. Make two rows of machine gathering stitches at the top edge of the pinned pieces: the first one ½ inch (1.3 cm) from the top edge, and the second row ¼ inch (6 mm) above the first line of stitching. Pull up the gathers evenly to create a circle 72 inches in diameter (182.8 cm).

3. Press open one folded edge of bias hem facing tape. Place the raw edge along the right side of the gathered gauze panels, keeping the top edges of the tape and the panels even. Pin the tape in place, and stitch it along the ½-inch (1.3 cm) seam that forms the bottom gathering line. Press the bias tape over, aligning its folded edge with the stitching line on the wrong side of the panels, to encase the raw edges of the panels. Stitch again along the folded edge of the tape to thoroughly encase the panels.

4. From the remaining gauze fabric, cut a yard (.9 m) of gauze in half. You should end up with two pieces that are approximately 18 inches (45.7 cm) wide and 54 inches (137.2 cm) long. Cut a 19-inch-long (48.3 cm) piece from one, and sew it to the other, creating a piece that's 73 inches (185.4 cm) long. This piece will form the top of the tent; set it aside.

Triangle Trim

1. From the yard (.9 m) of heavier-weight fabric, cut three equal pieces, each measuring 12 x 54 inches (30.5 x 137.2 cm).

2. Out of one of the three pieces, cut two 20-inch (50.8 cm) pieces. (The remaining 14 inches [35.6 cm] of that piece are scrap.) Sew one 20-inch (50.8 cm) piece to one 54-inch (137.2 cm) piece, using a ½-inch (1.3 cm) seam allowance. Repeat the process with the other two pieces. When you finish, you should have two 73-inch (185.4 cm) pieces. One will serve as the facing for the other.

3. To determine the triangle points, lay one of your strips on a flat surface, wrong side of the fabric up. Reserve ½ inch (1.3 cm) on each end for sewing in a seam, then measure off six 12-inch (30.5 cm) sections. Divide each section in half, ending up with twelve 6-inch (15.2 cm) sections. On each 6-inch (15.2 cm) section line, make a mark 5 inches (12.7 cm) up from the bottom edge. About ¼ inch (6 mm) up from the bottom edge, mark the centers of each section (every 3 inches [7.6 cm]). Using a straightedge, draw lines from the center marks up to the 5-inch (12.7 cm) marks, creating your 12 triangle points (see figure 1, page 86).

4. Pin your facing to the top piece of fabric, right sides together, and stitch along the lines you drew to form the triangles. Trim the seam to ¼ inch (6 mm), and clip the seams to the stitching line at the upper corners of the triangles.

5. Turn the piece right side out, using the end of the sharpened dowel to push the points of the triangles out smoothly. Press the piece.

6. With the right sides together, pin the ends of the piece together (forming a circle). Beginning at what will be the top edge of the circle, use a ½-inch (1.3 cm) seam allowance, and stitch down ½ inch (1.3 cm). Back tack, then leave the next ½ inch (1.3 cm) of seam free of stitches. After the unstitched space, back tack again and finish stitching the seam to the bottom edge (see figure 2). The opening you left is where you'll insert the hanging cord later. Press the seam open, and turn the piece right side out.

Assembly

1. On the gauze piece you created to form the top of the tent, stitch the short sides together, using a ½-inch (1.3 cm) seam allowance, and leaving a ½-inch (1.3 cm) opening. Begin at the top edge, stitch 1 inch (2.5 cm), back tack, leave ½ inch (1.3 cm) unstitched, back tack again, then continue stitching. Press the seam open. Place the wrong sides of this piece and the triangle trim piece together, match the seam lines, and pin the gauze piece to the top of the triangle trim piece. Stitch, using a ¼-inch (6 mm) seam allowance (see figure 3).

2. To make a casing for inserting the copper wire, fold the triangle trim piece along the seam line you just stitched, right sides of the fabric now together, and stitch again 1 inch (2.5 cm) from the folded edge. Press the casing toward the triangle trim piece (see figure 4).

3. Pin the bias-taped edge of gathered gauze panels to the back side of the bottom edge of the casing you just sewed. Stitch the pieces together close to the edge.

4. To make a casing for inserting the cord at the top of the gauze piece, turn the unfinished edge at the top of the piece under 1 inch (2.5 cm), press, and fold again inside the folded edge to create a finished ½-inch (1.3 cm) double hem. Stitch along the folded edge.

5. Insert the cord into the casing, using a bodkin. Pull the cord up taut (as you would the cord on a drawstring bag), tie it off with a double knot, and make a secure loop at the top for hanging the tent from a hook in the ceiling.

6. Insert the copper wire into the casing you created in the triangle trim piece, just above where you sewed the gathered panels. Use the pliers to shape the wire into a circle after you've inserted it. Tape the ends of the casing together, if necessary, and slipstitch the opening closed.

7. Install a strong hook in the ceiling where you want the tent to suspend, and hook the cord loop securely over it. The ends of the gathered panels should puddle on the floor.

FIGURE 1

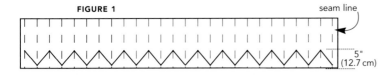

seam line

5" (12.7 cm)

FIGURE 2

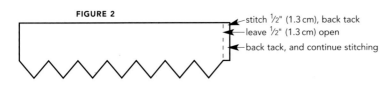

stitch ½" (1.3 cm), back tack
leave ½" (1.3 cm) open
back tack, and continue stitching

FIGURE 3

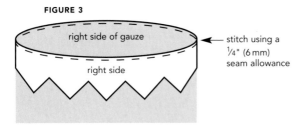

right side of gauze

right side

stitch using a ¼" (6 mm) seam allowance

FIGURE 4

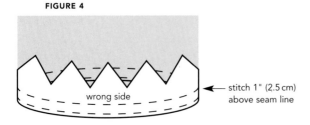

wrong side

stitch 1" (2.5 cm) above seam line

chalk
drawings

You brush on the chalkboard paint. Let them draw on the rest of the design—and erase and draw and erase and draw. One coat of this commercially available paint is typically all you need to transform the side of a night table, the panel of a door, or a section of wall into a full-blown blackboard. When they're tired of the idea, simply paint back over it with standard paint.

paint-in-place rug

In praise of painted rugs: they offer a smooth surface for wheeling around toy vehicles, they never bunch up and trip tiny feet, they stay right where you put them, and they're a breeze to wash. Best of all, you can create them in glorious splashes of color.

PAINT-IN-PLACE RUG *step-by-step*

MATERIALS & TOOLS

- Colored pencils or acrylic craft paints, paper, and pencil (for planning designs, colors, and patterns)
- Latex primer
- Eggshell (flat satin) latex paint in several colors, such as salmon or peach, pale yellow, light green, sky blue, pink, and orange
- Cellulose sponge, foam, or other material made for cutting your own stamp patterns
- Wooden blocks (various sizes)
- Contact cement
- Clear floor varnish in matt or satin finish
- Framing square and tape measure or straightedge ruler
- Pencil
- Low-tack painter's tape
- Sandpaper
- Tack cloth
- Various-sized rollers (You can use seam rollers or stencil rollers, as well as any other roller that will hold paint.)
- Glass plates or plates made from polystyrene foam (to use as palettes)
- Paint tray
- Various decorative artist's brushes, including flat and round
- Premade stencils and/or foam stamps (optional)
- Scissors
- Craft knife
- Foam brushes in various widths
- Stencil brushes (if you're using stencils)
- Paper towels or newsprint (to use as a blotter for stamps and/or blocks)
- Paint pad (optional)

INSTRUCTIONS

Painting the Rug Base

1. Work out ideas for color combinations and design elements on paper. Use colored pencils and/or craft paints to help create a loose formula.

2. Map out the area on the floor to become the rug. Use the framing square and pencil to mark off the corners and the measuring tape or ruler to mark off the internal dimensions. Mask off the outside dimensions of the rug, using low-tack painter's tape.

3. Make sure that the floor is free of all dust, grease, or grime. Use a tack cloth to remove any dust before applying paint.

4. Prime the floor inside the taped area. Allow it to dry thoroughly.

5. Using various widths of foam brushes and rollers, paint out stripes of various colors inside the taped lines. You can either use the paint tray or the glass or foam plates to contain your paints as you work. If you want to create very straight and uniform lines, use painter's tape to mask off the stripes. Otherwise paint free-form stripes, butting one against another. You may want to wait for one color to dry before adding the next, so the colors won't bleed into each other.

Adding Stamped or Stenciled Designs

You have several options for adding accents to your rug's stripes and border. You can purchase stamps or stencils that feature images similar to the ones we used here: a folk-art (uneven) heart, a flower with six round petals and a round center, a large insect, a simple leaf shape, a

large single flower shape, a round shape for polka dots, and a large and small square. You can also purchase other stamps or stencils that coordinate with your room's decor. Or, you can create your own stamps, following the first two steps below.

1. To create a stamp for a one-piece design (such as a heart), first draw your design on paper and cut out the paper template. Place the template on a piece of cellulose sponge or foam, and trace around it. Cut around the outline to create your stamp. To make the stamp easier to handle, glue it to a small block of wood. For other shapes that may not be so unwieldy, such as a simple leaf, you can cut the shape out of foam or sponge and use it without mounting it onto wood.

2. To create stamps of designs such as the insect or the six-petaled flower, shown here, draw out the design, breaking it up into components that, when combined, create the whole. Cut out all of the individual elements from the foam and then glue the pieces onto a wooden block to create the whole design (see figure 1).

3. Whether your stamps are purchased or handmade, use a brush or roller to load one with paint. Experiment with the stamp on paper first. Use an even pressure over the entire stamp, being careful not to rock back and forth so as not to blur the design. Also, practice lifting the block cleanly up and away from the surface.

4. Stamp all the designs onto the floor, referring to the photo for general placement or using your own original plans. Use one brush or roller per color.

5. When the stamped images are dry, use various brushes to create freehand embellishments, including long wavy lines, squiggle shapes, small hearts, small dots, outlines, and highlights (such as the lines around the hearts and the highlights inside the insects' bodies, shown here).

6. When all the paint is dry, gently peel off the painter's tape from the outer border of the rug. Use the larger square block to create a checkerboard design around the entire rug.

7. To seal and protect the floor, apply several coats of varnish using a roller or paint pad. Sand lightly in between coats, removing residue with a tack cloth between applications.

FIGURE 1. If you're making your own stamps, cut out the individual design elements, then glue the pieces onto a wooden block.

magic carpets

Sample squares and remnant strips from carpet stores can become decorative floor covers as well as launching pads for fun and games. All you need to transform them are a few bright strokes of paint.

Start with low-pile carpet pieces. Sketch on your design with a pencil or pale marker—think hopscotch squares, checkerboard patterns, and maps of your little one's favorite spots. Then, use acrylic or fabric paint to bring the design to life. Rubber stamps dipped in paint are also good carpet-decorating devices.

STOW
IT
AWAY
7

Never mind *how* such tiny beings can accumulate so much stuff. Better to face the fact that they can. And do. And you have to put it all someplace. Following are some clever ideas for where.

bed pockets

The items are different: storybooks versus the daily news, teddy bears instead of alarm clocks. Still, kids need bedside storage as much as adults do. These cozy, pocketed covers slip over headboards or footboards to keep all the essentials within easy reach.

BED POCKETS *step-by-step*

MATERIALS & TOOLS

- Decorator fabric, medium weight and at least 54 inches (137.2 cm) wide (Here's a gauge for the amount you need. A twin-size headboard that extends 20 inches [50.8 cm] above the mattress top and is a standard 38 inches [96.5 cm] wide will require 2 yards [1.8 m] of fabric.)
- Upholstery weight thread
- 1⅓ yard (1 m) polyester batting (This comes very wide, usually 60 inches [152.4 cm].)

- Standard measuring and marking tools
- Scissors
- Iron
- Sewing machine
- Straight pins
- Heavy-duty (suitable for denim) sewing machine needle
- Large hand-sewing needle

INSTRUCTIONS

1. Measure the height and width of your headboard or footboard. (Measure from the top of the mattress to the top of the board.) Add 4 inches (10.2 cm) to the width measurement and 10 to 12 inches (25.4 to 30.5 cm) to the height measurement. Using the dimensions you come up with, cut two pieces of fabric.

2. Cut another piece measuring 12 x 54 inches (30.5 x 137.2 cm). This piece will be sewn into four pockets.

3. On the pocket piece, press all the edges under 1 inch (2.5 cm), then press and fold again inside the folded edge to create a finished ½-inch (1.3 cm) double hem. Stitch along the folded edge on one long side only (this side will become the top edge of the pockets).

4. See figure 1, page 94, for the placement of the pleats you need to stitch to create the four 9-inch (22.9 cm) pockets. Make the folds, then, to define the edges of each pocket, topstitch very close to the folded edges (figure 2, page 94).

5. Position the pocket piece on the front of one of the pieces you cut in step 1. Place it approximately 3 inches (7.6 cm) below the top edge, and match the centers. Pin it in place.

6. Stitch through the center of each pleated area to define the pockets (see figure 3). Start each line by stitching a reinforcing triangle at the top edge. Also, stitch down the two sides.

7. Along the bottom, tuck in all the pleats that form the pockets, so the edges you topstitched along lie flat. Using a heavy-duty sewing machine needle and upholstery-weight thread, stitch across the bottom.

8. Drape the polyester batting over your headboard or footboard, with the folded edge of the batting along the top of the board. Trim any excess batting from the sides; you need only enough to pin the two sides together. Hand-stitch the sides together, using a large needle and upholstery weight thread. Make sure the batting extends below the top of the mattress a bit. Slip the sewn batting piece off temporarily.

9. Place the right sides of the headboard or footboard pieces together, and use a few pins across the top edge. Leaving the pinned piece wrong side out, slip it over the top of the headboard or footboard, and continue to pin the piece across the top, easing in any fullness with tucks or pleats at the outer edges. Pin down the sides, making sure the piece isn't too snug. (Remember it has to fit over the batting eventually.) Don't pin all the way down to the bottom; leaving a small slit on each side will make it easier to slip the finished piece on the headboard or footboard.

10. Remove the piece and stitch it together, removing pins as you go. Trim the seam. To finish the bottom and side edges, press them under 1 inch (2.5 cm), then press and fold again inside the folded edge to create a finished ½-inch (1.3 cm) double hem. Stitch along the folded edge. Turn the piece right side out.

11. Fit the batting over the headboard or footboard, and slip the pocketed cover on top of it.

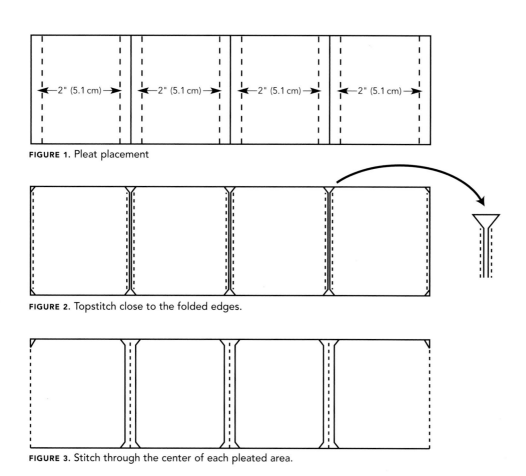

FIGURE 1. Pleat placement

FIGURE 2. Topstitch close to the folded edges.

FIGURE 3. Stitch through the center of each pleated area.

bag it

Nothing like a sturdy storage tote or two—or more. Group them in multiples and hang them from hooks, one for each child or sport or category of toy. There's an added bonus if you make bags as distinctive as the ones shown here. When they occasionally break free from their hooks and go places (sleepovers, summer camp, etc.), they just might make it back home.

MATERIALS & TOOLS

- 3 colors of fabric 60 inches (152.4 cm) wide, ⅝ yard (.6 m) of each
- Fusible web (approximately one 12-inch [30.5 cm] square per appliqué)
- Mercerized cotton thread in a color that coordinates with your fabric
- 2 lengths of ribbon, each 6 inches (15.2 cm) long
- 2 lengths of cord, each 1½ yards (1.4 m) long
- Standard measuring and marking tools
- Scissors
- Straight pins
- Sewing machine
- Iron
- Bodkin (a tweezer-like tool you'll use to insert the cord in its casing)

INSTRUCTIONS

1. Cut two rectangles of fabric (each a different color), measuring 20 x 12 inches (50.8 x 30.5 cm) for the front and back of the bag.

2. Cut one rectangle out of the third color of fabric measuring 9 x 12 inches (22.9 x 30.5 cm) for the bottom of the bag.

3. Cut two rectangles out of the third color of fabric measuring 9 x 20 inches (22.9 x 50.8 cm) for the sides of the bag.

4. Apply fusible web, according to the manufacturer's directions, to scrap squares of fabric. Working freehand or using patterns, draw numbers, letters, or other figures onto the fabric scraps, cut them out, peel the backing off the fusible web, and apply the figures to the front of the bag.

5. Pin the 9-inch (22.9 cm) side of one side piece to the 9-inch (22.9 cm) side of the bottom piece. Stitch the pieces together using a ½-inch (1.3 cm) seam allowance, then repeat on the other edge.

6. Pin the front piece to the piece you assembled in step 5, right sides together, and carefully clip a scant ½ inch (1.3 cm) of the seam so you can easily stitch the turns at the corners. Stitch the pieces together, using a ½-inch (1.3 cm) seam allowance. Repeat the process to stitch on the back piece.

7. Press the seams open as far down as possible.

8. Make a machine buttonhole in the two side pieces, 6 inches (15.2 cm) down from the top edge and centered horizontally on the piece. (You'll use these holes to insert the drawstring cord later.)

9. To make a casing for the cord on the top edge of the bag, fold 3½ inches (8.9 cm) of fabric to the wrong side of the bag, press the fold, turn the bottom edge under ½ inch (1.3 cm), press again, pin the bottom fold, and stitch close to the bottom folded edge all around. Stitch a second line all around 1 inch (2.5 cm) above the first line of stitching.

10. Turn the raw ends of each piece of ribbon trim under to create tabs. Hand-sew or machine stitch a tab to the center front and center back of the bag, stitching right at the edge of the top row of casing stitching, but not into the casing area.

11. Using the bodkin, insert one piece of cord into one of the buttonholes, guide it all the way around, and bring it back out the same buttonhole. Tie the ends together. Repeat the process using the other cord and the second buttonhole. Pull up the ends to draw up the bag.

BAG WITH GROMMETS *step-by-step*

MATERIALS & TOOLS

- ⅝ yard (.56 m) fabric
- 1 yard (.9 m) medium-weight iron-on interfacing (for stiffening bands and bottom)
- Mercerized cotton thread in coordinating color
- Grommets
- 1 yard (.9 m) cord for drawstring
- Standard measuring and marking tools
- Scissors
- Iron
- Sewing machine
- Straight pins
- Grommet tool

INSTRUCTIONS

1. Cut one piece of fabric for the body of the bag measuring 15 x 32 inches (38.1 x 81.3 cm). Cut two upper bands (one will serve as facing for the other) and one lower band, each measuring 3 x 32 inches (7.6 x 81.3 cm). Cut one round piece for the bottom of the bag measuring 10¼ inches (26 cm) in diameter. Cut one loop for the bag to hang by that measures 8 x 4 inches (20.3 x 10.2 cm).

2. Cut interfacing pieces the same size as the bands and the bottom piece. Apply it according to the manufacturer's directions.

3. Stay stitch ½ inch (1.3 cm) in from the raw edge on one long side of the bottom band. (This is a reinforcing stitching; you'll clip up to this line to fit the band around the round bottom piece later.)

4. Pin one long edge of the body of the bag to the unstitched long edge of the bottom band, right sides together, and stitch, using a ½-inch (1.3 cm) seam allowance.

5. Pin one long edge of one upper band to the other long edge of the body of the bag, right sides together, and stitch, using a ½-inch (1.3 cm) seam allowance. Press the seams toward the bands, and topstitch close to the seam line.

6. Pin the sides of the body-band piece together, matching the seam lines, and stitch using a ½-inch (1.3 cm) seam allowance. Press the seam open.

7. Fold the circular bottom piece in half, and mark the fold points with pins on each side. On the lower band of the bag, mark the spot directly opposite the seam with a pin (so the seam and the pin mark the piece's halfway points). Right sides together, match the pins on the bottom piece with the halfway points on the band. Clip to the stay stitching on the lower band just to the reinforcing line you stitched in step 3, and pin the bottom circle into place, easing to fit. Stitch, using a ½-inch (1.3 cm) seam allowance, right on top of the reinforcing line.

8. To create the hanging loop, fold the loop piece in half, wrong sides together, press under ½ inch (1.3 cm) on both long sides, and stitch the sides together close to the edges. Pin the short edges centered over the seam of the bag's upper band. Stitch the ends in place.

9. Fold the remaining upper band, which will serve as facing for the one already in place, in half and stitch the ends together, using a ½-inch (1.3 cm) seam allowance. Matching the seams, pin the right sides of the two upper bands together. Stitch along the top edge using a ½-inch (1.3 cm) seam allowance. It's a good idea to do some extra stitching over the loop ends you sewed on in step 8. Press the seam toward the body of the bag, then flip the facing over and press it to the inside. Press under a ½-inch (1.3 cm) seam, covering the seam where the body of the bag connects to the outer upper band. Carefully topstitch along the seam line to hold the facing in place. Also, topstitch the top edge of the outer band, close to the folded edge.

10. Using the grommet tool, place 12 large grommets evenly around the top band of the bag. Weave the cord through the grommets for a drawstring, and knot the ends of the cord.

little ledges

There's a cardinal rule about storage space in kids' rooms: every little bit counts. A decorative chair rail that juts out from the wall, for example, is also a useful ledge that can hold toy trains, sports trophies, or a family of dolls. And here's the really good news. If your wall doesn't happen to feature such a ledge, adding one is easy.

LITTLE LEDGES *step-by-step*

MATERIALS & TOOLS

- Brick molding
- 1 x 4 board
- Lengths of backbend molding for ledge lip
- Acrylic paint (or other finishing materials)
- Finishing nails
- Wood screws
- Sandpaper
- Paintbrush
- Level
- Measuring tools
- Hammer
- Electric drill and bit to fit screws

INSTRUCTIONS

1. Finish sand and paint or otherwise finish your molding pieces before hanging them.

2. Use a level to hang your brick molding with finishing nails.

3. Screw the 1 x 4 board (which becomes your ledge) on top of the brick molding (see figure 1).

4. Use small finishing nails to attach the lip piece to the ledge.

FIGURE 1
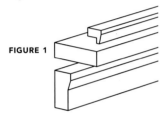

full coverage

No matter how many other inventive ideas you come up with, you'll likely find that good old-fashioned storage shelves are still an indispensable part of the attempt to keep everything in your child's room in its place. No need for them to be dreary and ordinary looking, though. Blend them right into the rest of the room's decor by covering them over with a colorful print.

MATERIALS & TOOLS

- Shelf paper that complements the room's colors and patterns (Try to purchase self-adhesive [and washable] shelf papers. If you can't find self-adhesive papers, you can mount any sort of paper or fabric using spray adhesive and slightly modifying the following instructions.)
- Ruler or yardstick
- Pencil
- Scissors

INSTRUCTIONS

1. If possible, remove your shelves. Measure their length, thickness, and depth. Measure and mark your shelf paper to equal the length, thickness, and twice the depth of the shelves. Add ¼ to ½ inch (6 mm to 1.3 cm) more to the depth measurement. Cut out the shelf paper.

2. Work on a hard, flat surface, such as a tabletop or the floor. Peel about 2 inches (5.1 cm) of the backing paper from one of the pieces of cut-out shelf paper. Carefully adhere the exposed area to one of the shelves, aligning the edges of the shelf paper along the back and side edges of the shelf.

3. Lift the shelf paper and peel off enough backing to cover the top of the shelf. Smooth the material to adhere it to the shelf. If necessary, peel up the shelf paper and realign it. Then, peel enough backing to wrap the paper around the thickness of the shelf.

4. Turn the shelf over and finish covering the opposite side. Adhere any excess paper to the back edge of the shelf. Trim the paper if necessary.

5. Repeat the process to cover your other shelves.

decorated desk drawers

Sooner or later, teething rings and rattles give way to colored pencils, construction paper, stamps, stickers, and books. A small, inexpensive desk unit offers a grown-up-feeling way to store these sorts of supplies. And swatches of shelf paper, wallpaper, or even fabric that pick up the room's colors or patterns can transform a desk's ordinary doors and drawers into decorative features.

MATERIALS & TOOLS

- Printed papers, self-adhesive shelf paper, or tightly woven fabrics
- Acrylic medium or white craft glue
- Polyurethane (optional)
- Sandpaper
- Ruler
- Pencil
- Scissors
- Craft knife
- Paintbrush

INSTRUCTIONS

1. Remove any drawer pulls from the drawers, and set the pulls and screws aside. (Storing them in a plastic bag is a good idea and will save you from frantic rummaging later on.)

2. Lightly sand the fronts of the drawers to roughen any paint or finish. This will give you a better surface for adhering your selected material.

3. Measure the height and width of each of your drawer fronts.

4. Measure and mark your selected material. Add ¼ inch (6 mm) to both of your measurements. Cut out the material with scissors.

5. If you're using self-adhesive paper, peel the backing and adhere the paper. Carefully smooth out any wrinkles that appear by lifting the paper and repositioning it. When the self-adhesive paper is smoothly adhered, trim any excess paper along the edges of the drawer with the craft knife.

6. If you're using paper or tightly woven fabric, brush a light, even coat of acrylic medium or white craft glue on the upper third of a drawer. Position the top third of the material and smooth out any wrinkles. Brush a light coat of medium or glue on the bottom portion of the drawer, and roll the material down the drawer front. Smooth the material and let it dry. Trim any excess with a craft knife.

7. Coat your covered drawer fronts with a light coat of acrylic medium or polyurethane, if you like.

cushioned toy box cover

Your kids are occasionally going to face tough decisions. The rubber ball or the plastic dinosaur?
Chinese checkers or pickup sticks? If they've got a basic wooden toy box, you can add a cushy,
comfy seat for them to lounge on while they ponder what to pull out next.

MATERIALS & TOOLS

- Polyester batting (Cut a piece measuring 1 inch [2.5 cm] less than the fabric piece on all sides.)
- Fabric (To determine how much, measure the length and width of your box lid, add the height of the sides, then add 2 inches [5.1 cm]. For example, if your lid measures 18 x 24 inches [45.7 x 61 cm] and its sides are 2 inches [5.1], you need a piece of fabric measuring 24 x 30 inches [61 x 76.2 cm].)
- Decorative ribbon trim at least 1 inch (2.5 cm) wide (You need 1 inch [2.5 cm] more than the perimeter measurement of your lid.)
- Standard measuring and marking tools
- Staple gun and staples
- Scissors
- Fabric glue
- Straight pins

INSTRUCTIONS

1. Place the batting on top of the lid and smooth it over the sides. Using the staple gun, place one staple in the center of each side to hold the batting in place. Cut away the excess batting at each corner, so the edges meet at the corners. Place one staple at each corner edge. Make sure the batting extends no farther than about 1 inch (2.5 cm) above the bottom edges of the sides of the lid.

2. Position the fabric evenly over the batting. Pull it taut at the sides, and place a staple in the center of each side.

3. To pleat the fabric at the corners, bring the fabric from one side (the shorter side if your lid isn't square) around the corner, smooth it, and staple it. Then fold the fabric from the adjacent side over, and staple it. Repeat the process on the other three corners. Position all your staples close to the bottom edge of the lid, so they'll be covered later with the ribbon trim.

4. Working on one side of the lid at a time, apply a bead of glue to the back of the ribbon trim and apply it to the bottom edge of the lid. Begin at one corner, wrap ½ inch (1.3 cm) of the ribbon around the corner edge to start, then press the glued ribbon firmly in place along that side, covering the fabric edge completely. Continue gluing the ribbon around the lid. When you come back to your starting point, fold the remaining ½ inch (1.3 cm) of ribbon under, and add some glue to the folded edge. You can use some straight pins to hold the trim in place until the glue dries.

gingham & stripe
etcetera drawers

Kids seem to need lots of etcetera spots—smallish holding places for private collections of rocks, notes passed from friends on the school bus, and various other specimens from the world around them. Here's a simple technique for covering the tiny drawer units and little cabinets they need with a cheery background design.

MATERIALS & TOOLS

- Latex primer
- White latex paint (satin or eggshell finish)
- Acrylic craft paint in light blue and medium blue (or other colors of your choice)
- Spray acrylic sealer or varnish
- Paintbrush or foam brush
- Straightedge ruler, triangle, or framing square
- Pencil
- Flat decorative artist brushes in different widths and/or a detail or liner brush
- Low-tack painter's tape (optional)

INSTRUCTIONS

You can paint gingham and stripe designs freehand, relying only on some general guide marks. Or, for a more uniform result, you can tape your lines off with painter's tape. Either way, prime the drawers first, then paint them with two coats of white paint and let them dry thoroughly.

Freehand Technique

Vertical Stripes

1. Work on one drawer at a time. Use a measuring tool and pencil to mark equidistant intervals across the drawer face. Make pencil marks on the top and bottom of the drawer. Use your straightedge to connect the pencil marks, leaving fine pencil lines to use as your guides for painting.

2. You'll want to use various brushes to create different widths of stripes. For the fine lines, use a detail or a liner brush or the chiseled edge of a flat brush. Load your brush with paint, center it on a pencil line, and use one smooth, steady, and even motion to pull the brush across the entire pencil line. Repeat the process to paint vertical stripes across the entire surface of the drawer.

Gingham Design

1. Make vertical stripes first, following the steps above but using a flat brush to create a wider line. Use your lighter paint color for these stripes.

2. When the vertical lines are dry, rotate the drawer and mark the horizontal spacing with the ruler and pencil. Use your darker paint to create the horizontal stripes.

Taping Technique

1. Make equidistant pencil lines, just as if you were using the freehand approach.

2. Working from right to left, place painter's tape to the left of the first pencil line. Paint your stripe to the right of the tape. Before the paint begins to dry, gently peel off the tape.

3. Repeat the taping and painting process, using a fresh piece of tape for each stripe. You can paint the gingham design in the same manner, but allow the vertical stripes to dry before painting the horizontals.

Whichever technique you use, spray on one or two coats of acrylic sealer or use varnish to protect the painted surfaces.

If you want to add a central design on top of your gingham and stripes (like the teddies, hearts, and dog shown here), paint on some simple freehand shapes, stamp or stencil your images in place, or clip design elements from a leftover scrap of the room's wallpaper, and glue them where you want them.

infant organizers

You've just set your bundle of joy down in his playpen or crib so you can grab a few precious moments of hands-free time. The last thing you want to spend those moments doing is running to the next room for the bottle, then back for the blanket, and back again for the right stuffed toy. These soft, pocketed organizers tie in place on the rails of playpens and cribs, keeping vital supplies in order—and right where you need them.

MATERIALS & TOOLS

- 5¼ yards (4.7 m) cotton duck or other sturdy fabric, 54 inches (137.2 cm) wide
- Mercerized cotton thread
- Fabric paint
- Standard measuring and marking tools
- Scissors
- Iron
- Sewing machine
- Bodkin (a tweezer-like tool helpful in turning pieces)
- Straight pins
- Sharpened dowel rod
- Fine-bristle brush
- Pressing cloth

INSTRUCTIONS

1. For the base pieces, measure and cut four pieces from the fabric, two measuring 27 x 27 inches (68.6 x 68.6 cm), and two measuring 27 x 48 inches (68.6 x 121.9 cm). (These pieces will give you organizers for all four sides of a playpen or crib.)

2. For the pockets, measure and cut six pieces measuring 14 x 50 inches (35.6 x 127 cm) and four pieces measuring 11 x 17 inches (27.9 x 43.2 cm).

3. For the ties, cut eight pieces measuring 6 x 18 inches (15.2 x 45.7 cm) and four pieces measuring 2½ x 12 inches (6.4 x 30.5 cm).

4. On each of the base pieces, press the edges under 1 inch (2.5 cm), then fold again inside the folded edge to create a finished ½-inch (1.3 cm) hem. Stitch around all four sides of all the pieces, close to the fold.

5. Make the large ties that attach the organizers to the playpen or crib. Fold each 6 x 18-inch (15.2 x 45.7 cm) piece in half lengthwise, right sides together, and stitch across each short end and down the long sides, using a ¼-inch (6 mm) seam allowance. Leave small openings in the centers of the long sides for turning. Using the bodkin, turn the pieces right side out, press them, and slip-stitch the opening closed by hand.

6. Pin a tie to the back sides of the upper corners of each base piece, and stitch several times to make sure the ties are firmly attached (see figure 1).

7. Create the smaller pockets. Fold each 11 x 17-inch (27.9 x 43.2 cm) piece in half, right sides together, to make pieces measuring 11 x 8½ inches (27.9 x 21.6 cm). Stitch around the three sides, leaving small openings for turning. Turn the pieces, push all the corners out using the sharpened end of the dowel rod, and press them.

8. To make small decorative ties for the fronts of the small pockets, use the 2½ x 12-inch (6.4 x 30.5 cm) pieces, and follow the instructions for making the large ties (step 5). Topstitch through the center of each to attach it to the front of the pocket, about 1 inch (2.5 cm) down from the top edge, then tie it in a knot.

9. Create the larger pockets with flaps. Fold each 14 x 50-inch (35.6 x 127 cm) piece in half, right sides together, to make pieces measuring 14 x 25 inches (35.6 x 63.5 cm). Round off the corners of the ends that will become the flaps (see figure 2). Pin and stitch the sides of the piece, using a ½-inch (1.3 cm) seam allowance and leaving a small opening for turning. Turn the pieces, push all the corners out using the sharpened end of the dowel rod, and press them, then fold over a 10-inch (25.4 cm) flap (your actual pockets are 15 inches [38.1 cm] high).

10. Before stitching the pockets in place, use fabric paint and the fine-bristle brush to make random strokes along the edges of the pockets, if you like. Allow the paint to dry completely, then set it with an iron and pressing cloth, following the manufacturer's instructions.

11. Using the photo as a guide, place your pockets on the base pieces and stitch them in place close to the edges on the sides and bottoms. On the large pockets, fold the flap up and out of the way while you're stitching, then lay it back down over the pocket.

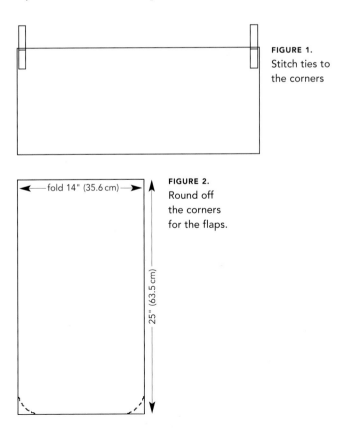

FIGURE 1.
Stitch ties to
the corners

FIGURE 2.
Round off
the corners
for the flaps.

fold 14" (35.6 cm)

25" (63.5 cm)

BASIC TECHNIQUES

Inspired but in need of a bit more direction? Here's an easy guide for tackling all the standard do-it-yourself tasks described throughout the book. Whether you want to brush up on painting techniques or learn the fundamentals of hanging wallpaper, this chapter gives you the information you need.

painting walls

One of the easiest and least expensive ways to transform an ordinary room into one that suits your young individual's budding sense of style is to cover the walls with a couple of coats of fresh paint.

PAINT

You've got two major types of paint to choose from: oil-based (alkyd) and water-based (latex). In most cases, latex is the way to go. Though alkyd paints may be slightly more damage resistant, latex paints today are plenty durable. They're also nontoxic, quick-drying, and they clean up with soap and water as opposed to mineral spirits. In addition, latex paints lend themselves well to added effects, such as sponging and stenciling, which we'll get to later in this section. Consider alkyd paints if you plan to also coat doors, window trim, or other accent spots that will need a hard finish that'll stand up to lots of washings.

Paints also come in different gloss ranges. The level of gloss affects the shine and brightness of your walls.

FLAT PAINTS, the most common kind for walls and ceilings, are easy on the eye, reflect little light, reduce glare, and help hide small imperfections.

EGGSHELL, LO-LUSTRE, and **SATIN PAINTS** are good for heavy-use areas that will be subjected to frequent washings. They have a slight sheen and hold up a bit better than flat paints.

SEMIGLOSS PAINTS are a popular choice for kids' rooms. They've got a slightly greater sheen and can handle a bit more wear and tear than satin paints.

GLOSS and **HIGH-GLOSS PAINTS,** also called enamels, dry to an extremely shiny finish, making them better for woodwork and furniture than entire walls. An enamel surface can withstand heavy use and scrubbing, but it will also reflect any surface imperfection.

SPECIALTY PAINTS: If you really want to make a statement, experiment with the new glitter, glow-in-the-dark, and chalkboard paints.

Estimating Quantity

To figure out how much paint you need, measure the perimeter of your room. Multiply the result by the ceiling height to get the total square feet or meters you need to cover with paint. Don't worry about deducting the space taken up by windows and doors unless they add up to more than 100 square feet ($9m^2$), which is unlikely when you're dealing with a child's room. Divide your total square feet or meters into the number of square feet or meters your paint can promises to cover. Round up to the nearest whole number to determine how many cans you need.

Choosing and Matching Colors

First, head to the paint store toting along whatever you want your paint to match, from bright toys and fabric samples to rolls of wallpaper and entire bedspreads. Pick out your paint samples, and take everything back home. Tack the samples in place on the wall, and pay attention to how they look at different times of day and under different lighting conditions. Narrow your choices to two or three paint colors, buy a small amount of each, and apply the paint to scraps of wood. Live with your larger color samples for a day or two before deciding which one you'll use to cover the whole room, remembering that the larger the final painted area, the stronger the color will seem.

MATERIALS & TOOLS

BRUSHES. Nylon or polyester brushes are best for latex paints. Use a natural-bristle brush with alkyd paints. Whichever bristle type you pick, you want brushes with contoured tops that form an oval or a rounded edge. They're best for the job at hand: cutting a fine line along trim and at corners where walls and ceilings meet.

DROP CLOTHS. Disposable plastic drop cloths protect flooring and furniture from paint splatters.

PAINT ROLLERS. Choose a roller with a heavy wire frame and a sturdy, threaded handle that extends (making it possible to easily reach the high spots). The painting surface of the roller is also called a sleeve or cover. It slides on and off the roller cage so you can clean and store it. The length of the nap on sleeves or covers varies; the more irregular your wall surface, the longer nap you'll need.

PRIMER. This specially formulated paint adheres well to bare surfaces and provides an inexpensive base for your more expensive topcoat to stick to.

ROLLER PAN. You need a shallow metal pan with a ramp. You'll run your roller up and down the ramp to evenly distribute the paint on the sleeve.

TRIM GUARD. Also called an edger, this handy hand-held tool lets you shield adjacent surfaces such as window glass or carpeting from the fresh paint you're applying to a wall. It's not essential, but it's a nice-to-have extra.

painting walls

LOOK OUT FOR LEAD

If your home is older, there's a good chance its walls (and molding and trim) were painted with lead paint, which can be dangerous to both pregnant women and children. You definitely want to remove it, but you want to take extra care when doing so. Sanding and scraping—techniques that can scatter paint chips and lead particles—are not the techniques to use. Check with a local paint supplier about the best products and methods for safely removing lead paint.

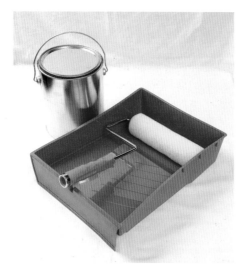

GENERAL TECHNIQUES

PREP YOUR WALLS. Typically, you can paint right over any surface, after quickly sponging off any dirt, dust, or mildew and letting it dry. But if the paint that's already on your walls is chipped and peeling, you may want to remove it so you've got a clean, smooth surface for your new paint. You can scrape it off, remove it with a heat gun, or strip it with solvents. You'll probably also want to remove old wallpaper. If you simply paint over it, it'll be nearly impossible to remove if you ever want to strip the room down to its bare walls in the future and start over. Also, remove the covers on electrical receptacles and light switches, cover electrical outlets with masking tape, and remove any heating grates or plate covers from your walls. Once your walls are ready, you can move onto priming and painting.

PRIME. Apply a coat of primer with a roller or brush. Choose the type that's right for your job; latex primers are for bare wood, while specially designed wallboard primer will seal the surface of new wallboard. If part of your purpose in painting is to cover over Crayon marks, felt-tip marker drawings, or other kid-related stains, prevent them from bleeding through by applying a stain blocker or white pigmented shellac. You can get it in a spray can if you need only a small amount. Make sure everything is completely dry before you move on.

PAINT. Two simple guidelines will make your paint job a success (and the process more enjoyable): work from top to bottom, and outline first then fill in second. If you're painting the room's ceiling in addition to the walls, start there. Move on to the walls, and end with door and window trim, doors, and finally baseboards. Use a brush first to outline all the areas a roller can't reach, such as corners, places where the wall meets trim, etc. When you're ready to roll, precondition your roller sleeve by rinsing it with water and spinning it until it's dry. (You don't need to precondition a lamb's-wool sleeve.) Fill one third of your paint tray with paint, load the roller in the deep end of the tray, and smooth it on the sloping end to evenly distribute the paint. Start at the top third of your walls, and work your way down, applying equal pressure and spreading the paint evenly. It's helpful to lay the paint on in the shape of an M or W, then fill in the blank spaces, working from the unpainted areas into the wet paint.

painting floors

If you've got a wooden floor that's seen better days, you've also got the perfect canvas for adding color, pattern, thematic design, even whimsy to your child's room.

PAINT

The folks at your local paint store should be able to help you choose the paint best suited for the type and condition of your wood floor. For high-traffic, heavy-use floors like those in kids' rooms, oil-based enamels offer the best durability. You can also find oil-based paint formulated especially for floors and porches, though it's available in only a limited range of colors.

MATERIALS & TOOLS

BRUSHES & ROLLER. The same painting tools you use on walls will work on floors.

FLOOR POLISHER. Tool-rental outlets and even the floor-care centers of many grocery stores rent polishers you can use to roughen up the surface of your floor.

VACUUM CLEANER. You need one to do what it does best: remove dirt and dust, plus sanding residue. A tack rag (basically sticky cheesecloth designed to pick up dust) is a more labor-intensive substitute.

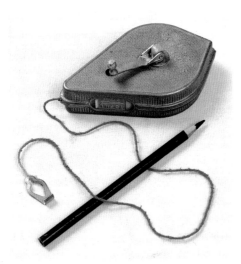

GENERAL TECHNIQUES

PREP YOUR FLOOR. Your floor must be free of any gloss or sheen before you apply the paint. Use the floor polisher to buff away the top surface and remove any dirt or grit in the process. When you're finished, use the vacuum to clean up your mess, focusing special attention on cracks and crevices between floorboards.

MARK YOUR PATTERN (OPTIONAL). If you're painting a design, map it out on graph paper first. Then, use measuring tools and a pencil to transfer the pattern to your floor. If your design features straight lines (a checkerboard pattern, for example), you can use a chalk line to snap the lines according to evenly spaced marks on the edges of the floor.

PAINT. Start by using a brush to outline the perimeter of the floor and to fill in any wide spaces or cracks between floorboards. Once you've got the edges painted, use the roller to fill in the rest of the floor. Working on an area that's about 24 inches (61 cm) wide at a time, paint the entire length of your floorboards, from one wall to the other, then move over to the next strip. Using the edge of a board as your stopping and starting point keeps your wet edge of paint on an even plane rather than in the middle of a board, where lap marks would be visible. Let your floor dry completely between coats if you're adding more than one. For added durability, finish with a couple of coats of matte-finish, non-yellowing polyurethane.

painting furniture

Often, the distinctive, delightful difference between a kid's room and every other room in the house is the bright red chest of drawers, the pale pink shelves, or the table and chairs that feature a polka-dot pattern. Paint is the perfect way to give any piece of furniture the color and flair it needs to fit into a kid-oriented atmosphere.

FURNITURE

You can start with already-painted furniture you plan to refinish or with new pieces of unfinished furniture. Flea markets, yard sales, and grandparents' attics are great sources for the former. Stores that specialize in unpainted furniture offer a wide selection of the latter, with pieces produced in sizes and styles especially for kids.

If you're purchasing unfinished furniture, solid-wood pieces are the best choice. While you can find unfinished furniture made of particle board, plywood, and veneers, solid-wood construction gives you a piece that is stronger, longer lasting, and a better investment. Medium-density fiberboard (MDF) is another option. Though it's weaker and more likely to chip than solid wood, it's popular with makers of children's furniture because it can be cut into a range of fanciful shapes that are smooth all over, even at the cut ends. Depending on where you purchase your unfinished furniture, it can come either assembled or unassembled. If it's unassembled, it should be accompanied by illustrated instructions and all the hardware you need to easily put your piece together.

PAINT

Just as when you're painting walls, you've got a choice between oil-based (alkyd) and water-based (latex) paints and flat, semigloss, and gloss sheens. Again, the advantage of latex paints is that they're nearly odorless, they clean up with soap and water, and they dry quickly. Alkyd paints, on the other hand, are more resistant to wear and tear. For added color options, you may also want to experiment with artist's acrylics, sold in tubes or jars. They're great for painting small areas, detailing a motif, outlining, and highlighting. Artist's acrylics are more concentrated than household paint, so you may want to thin them with water before using them.

MATERIALS & TOOLS

BRUSHES. You probably don't need to invest in specialized decorative painting brushes. A 2-inch (5.1 cm) or 3-inch (7.6 cm) flat paintbrush used for household painting is versatile enough to handle most jobs. A straight-edge brush works well on flat surfaces; an angled brush will be handier when you want to paint clean, straight lines and nice sharp corners. For detail work such as outlining, highlighting, or blending, you'll want a selection of small artist's brushes.

CARBON or **GRAPHITE TRANSFER PAPER.** You'll need this if you're transferring a design to the surface of your furniture.

DROP CLOTHS. They provide a protective layer between your painting project and your floor. Use an old sheet, purchase an inexpensive plastic cloth, or spread out old newspapers.

GLAZE MEDIUM. Formulated to dry more slowly than paint, glaze medium gives you a longer working time for techniques that call for manipulation of the top coat of paint, such as rag rolling or stippling. It comes in either water- or oil-based formulas and dries clear.

PRIMERS. If you're working on unfinished furniture, you need a primer to fill and seal the bare wood so the surface will better accept your paint. Choose a good all-purpose primer-sealer formulated for use with water- or oil-based paints.

RAGS. Lint-free rags are indispensable when it comes to wiping up drips and spills and for cleaning your brushes.

SANDPAPER. Sandpaper is categorized by its grade (coarse, medium, fine, and extra fine) or by a number that indicates the amount of grit used per square inch on the sanding surface (#150 to #200 are considered medium grade, for example).

TACK CLOTH. You'll use this sticky cloth to clean your wood's surface, removing debris and sanding residue before you paint.

VARNISHES & PROTECTIVE COATS. If you want to give your painted surface extra protection, add sheen, or tone down a too-shiny surface, you can apply a few top coats of clear varnish or polyurethane. Varnishes come in water- and oil-based formulas and in sheens ranging from matte to high-gloss.

WOOD FILLER. If your piece features small dents or nicks, natural flaws, or nail or staple holes, use wood filler to even the surface before applying your primer or first coat of paint.

Whether you're painting unfinished or already-painted furniture, try to work in a space that's free of drafts and airborne dirt, so specks of dust and lint will be less likely to land on your just-painted surfaces.

Painting Unfinished Furniture

1. Fill any holes or indentations with wood filler, following the manufacturer's instructions for application and drying time.

2. Once the filler is dry, use a fine-grit sandpaper to remove any excess filler and to buff your entire piece.

3. Use the tack cloth to remove any sanding debris.

4. Seal the wood with a coat of primer. Once it's dry, sand again, and again use the tack cloth to remove any debris.

5. Apply your first coat of paint, let it dry, sand your piece again, and wipe it clean.

6. Add your top coat, let it dry, then finish with several coats of varnish if you like.

Painting Already-Painted Furniture

If the existing paint on your piece of furniture is in good condition, just sand the piece thoroughly with medium-grade sandpaper and apply your new paint. If it features a few chips and cracks, sand the damaged areas smooth before painting. For pieces with more damaged existing paint, use wood filler to even out the nicks and gaps, let it dry, sand it smooth, then apply a coat of primer before adding your paint. It's a good idea, in this case, to apply two coats of your finish paint, sanding between the first and second coat.

surface decoration techniques

There are a number of simple, standard techniques for adding pattern, texture, and splashes of colorful design to your painted surfaces.

STENCILING

Stenciling is simply painting through a hole (or pattern of holes) cut in a piece of stencil material that you've taped against your surface. All you need is a stencil (the pattern of cutout holes), paint (acrylic is most common; specialty stencil paints and paint sticks and crayons are also available), and a tool for applying the color (artist's brushes, stencil brushes, and sponges are all options). Precut stencils in every design motif imaginable are available at craft stores. You can also design your own stencils and cut them out of a water-resistant material, such as acetate.

BASIC STEPS FOR STENCILING:

1. Use painter's tape or spray adhesive to fix your stencils in place. If you're creating a room border or another design that must be perfectly placed, use a carpenter's level to draw a line you can use to align the edges of your stencils as you position them.

2. Dab on paint to fill the stencil's cutout area. Different brushing techniques produce different effects.

- *Dry-brush application,* which involves blotting your brush on a paper towel before applying the paint, creates a soft, muted result.

- *Stippling,* or applying the paint in a quick up-and-down motion, creates a fine, textural effect.

- *Swirling,* a method of applying a small amount of paint in a downward, twisting motion, creates a smooth finish with dark and light gradations.

Don't ever drag your brush over the stencil; you risk driving paint under the stencil and outside the design's border.

3. Gently remove the stencils, being careful not to smudge the painted design as you do.

SPONGING

Sponging is one of the simplest ways to texturize a surface with paint—a little dipping, a little patting, and you've got interesting patches of color that can serve as your final finish or as a background for additional treatments. Sponging is also a versatile technique. Use a soft touch, and the look is luminous. Apply more pressure and contact to intensify the color in specific areas, and you can create different shades of color. Or, blend several colors into each other, and you end up with a graduated effect. You can use sponges to produce uniform design elements, too; cut dots, diamonds, or any other basic shape from sponges, then use them to stamp your surface.

Kitchen sponges, cosmetic sponges, sea sponges, and sponge mitts all create interesting finishes. You can also "sponge" on paint with everything from crumpled newspaper to nubby fabric—all with their own imaginative effects.

STAMPING

A close cousin of sponging, stamping is another nearly effortless way to add painted accents to any surface. Rubber stamps come in an array of sizes and in designs ranging from spirals and stars to all the letters of the alphabet. You can use them to make cows jump over moons, fireflies buzz around light fixtures, or ballerinas dance along a chair rail. Simply dip your stamp in acrylic paint and press it against the surface you want to decorate.

STENCILING

SPONGING

STAMPING

RAG ROLLING

COMBING

RAG ROLLING

Give the surface you're decorating a luxurious, mottled look with a technique known as rag rolling. It's best if you can plan enough time to complete your entire piece (or room) in one session when you're rag rolling, rather than stopping midstream and coming back to it. Also, since you need to work fairly quickly, you'll be less harried and have more fun if you can enlist the help of a painting partner.

BASIC STEPS FOR RAG ROLLING:

1. Choose two complementary paint colors for your surface. Use glossy or semi-gloss paint; they're absorbed less easily by walls and rags.

2. Prepare a set of rags by twisting fabric into 6-inch-long (15.2 cm) rolls. Any cloth will do, from old sheets and cloth diapers to burlap or worn-out dish towels. Be sure you prepare enough rolls to complete your furniture piece or your room. For an average-sized room (about 12 x 14 feet [3.7 x 4.3 m]) you'll need to tear up the equivalent of a double-bed sheet.

3. Apply the lighter color of paint to your surface, and let it dry completely.

4. Apply your second color of paint. While it's still wet, roll a rag lightly over the surface, holding the rag at both ends and working from top to bottom. The action removes parts of the top color, exposing the base color underneath.

5. Change your rolling direction often to add interest to the surface, and switch to a new rag each time the one you're working with becomes saturated.

COMBING

Create cross-hatch patterns, squiggly lines, and various other fun effects by using purchased or homemade tools to comb through one layer of paint and reveal another underneath. Triangular-shaped combing tools, available at craft stores, feature grooves on each side that have different weights and textures. You can also make a combing tool of your own by cutting "teeth" in the rubber blade of a squeegee or in a strip of cardboard. If you're combing a large area (all the walls of a room, for example), as with rag rolling, the process will go more smoothly if you've got a painting partner to help you.

BASIC STEPS FOR COMBING:

1. Choose two complementary paint colors for your surface. Flat paint is usually easier to work with than semigloss and high-gloss paints, which create a surface that's somewhat slick.

2. Apply your first layer of paint, and let it dry completely.

3. Apply your second color of paint. While it's still wet, pull your combing tool across the surface. It's a good idea to plan which way you'll comb before you begin. In general, if you're working on walls, begin in one corner and work your way down and across. Make long, clean strokes, and wipe your comb clean after each run.

wallpapering

Whether you want to cover entire walls or just add an easy accent border, wallpaper is a popular way to customize kids' rooms.

WALLPAPER TYPES

Save grass cloth, embossed wall coverings, and delicate hand-painted wallpapers for other parts of the house. For kids' rooms, vinyl wall coverings—which stand up to washing and scrubbing—are your best bet.

PAPER-BACKED VINYL is not only washable and sturdy, it's also generally peelable, so it's not terrifically hard to remove when your 10-year-old tells you choo choo trains are passé. It also typically comes in an easy-to-apply prepasted form. Best of all, paper-backed vinyl is available in tons of patterns designed with kids in mind.

FABRIC-BACKED VINYL is a bit more durable than paper-backed vinyl, but it's typically not prepasted.

VINYL-COATED PAPER is the least expensive option, but it's also the least durable. Sticky hands, Crayons, and the like will leave permanent marks.

Estimating Quantity

Using the same system described for estimating the quantity of paint (page 111), figure the total square feet or meters of your room's wall space. Divide your total by the square feet or meters a roll of the wallpaper you've chosen promises to cover. You probably won't come out with an even number; round up to determine how many rolls you should buy.

Go figure: Nobody knows why, but although wallpaper is priced by the single roll, it's sold only in packages of double rolls—a good thing to know when you're estimating how much you need to buy.

MATERIALS & TOOLS

BUCKET & SPONGE. You'll use these as you hang your paper to remove any wallpaper paste oozing from the edges of your newly applied paper.

LADDER. An obvious necessity if you're papering from ceiling to floor.

LEVEL. Anytime you need to determine a straight vertical or horizontal line on your walls, you'll need a level.

PAINT ROLLER OR PASTE BRUSH. If you're not working with prepasted wallpaper, you'll need one of these tools to apply adhesive to the back of your paper.

PLUMB LINE. Simply a weight attached to the end of a string, this tool helps you establish a straight vertical layout line. Tie the string to a nail near the top of the wall so the weight is just above the floor. When the line stops swinging, align a ruler with the string to mark your layout line.

RAZOR KNIFE. Use a razor knife with breakaway blades to trim off excess paper at ceiling and floor molding, light fixtures, etc.

SCISSORS. You'll use them to cut your wallpaper strips to size.

SEAM ROLLER. A seam roller is indispensable when it comes to pressing down the seams where two pieces of wallpaper meet.

SMOOTHING BRUSH. The flexible bristles on this brush help you smooth your hung paper so it's free of bubbles and wrinkles.

TAPE MEASURE. When you're measuring and cutting your paper, you've got to have one.

TRIM GUIDE. A painting edger or a broad knife can serve as a trim guide. You'll use is to press your wet wallpaper into a ceiling or wall joint before you trim it.

WATER TRAY. If you're using prepasted wallpaper, you'll need to soak it before hanging it.

GENERAL TECHNIQUES

PREP YOUR WALLS. Give your walls a good washing down and dry them well, patch any holes or cracks with wall compound, and, after the compound is dry, sand the patched areas until they're smooth. Also, remove the covers on electrical receptacles and light switches, cover electrical outlets with masking tape, and remove any heating grates or plate covers from your walls. If you like to follow all the rules, apply a coat of primer to your walls. Primer is only a must if you're papering over new drywall, but it'll promote adhesion on any type of wall and also make it easier to one day strip your paper. Finally, apply a coat of wallpaper sizing, a treatment that makes your walls tacky so the wallpaper paste or adhesive has something to bond with.

HANG THE PAPER. Use a level or plumb line to lay out a straight, vertical starting point on your wall. Cut your first strip of wallpaper from the roll. You want your strip a little longer than your wall is tall; you'll trim it later. Soak your strip in water, following your paper manufacturer's instructions, or apply wallpaper paste to the strip. Position the strip at the ceiling joint of the wall, leaving a few extra inches at the top, and carefully align one side with your starting line. Use your hands and the smoothing brush to smooth the strip in place, starting at the top and working down. Once the strip is straight, continue brushing to remove any wrinkles or bubbles. Hang subsequent strips the same way, carefully aligning the seams and using the seam roller to press them in place. As you go, use a wet sponge to wipe up any paste that oozes out of the seams.

TRIM. Where your wallpaper strips meet the ceiling, floor, or any trim, hold the trim guide in the joint, and use the razor knife to cut away the excess paper.

BORDERS

Not ready to tackle an entire wall? Hanging a border is an excellent (and easy) way to test your interest in wallpapering—and it may add all the decorative accent you need. Plenty of wallpaper manufacturers today sell both papers and borders designed especially for kids. Some specialty borders feature patterns designed to coordinate with bedding. Others are extra wide (filling up to 30 inches [76.2 cm] of wall space), and function as wall murals. You can hang a border in its traditional spot along the tops of your walls, use it to trim windows and doors, or even hang it at kid level, where it serves as a decorative chair rail.

Added benefit: When your child outgrows a certain pattern or theme, it's much easier to remove or replace a border than it is to repaper all the walls.

embroidered animal mobile, *page 24*

stenciled menagerie, *page 26*

PATTERNS:

star light, *page 37*

PATTERNS:

soft sculpture flowers, *page 41*

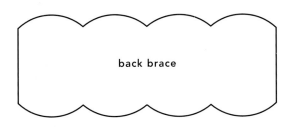

back brace

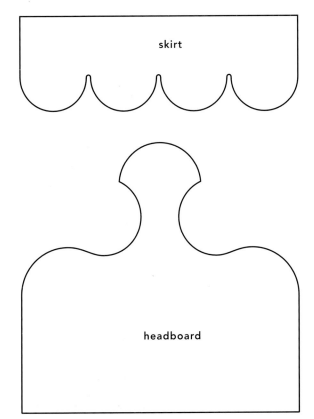

skirt

headboard

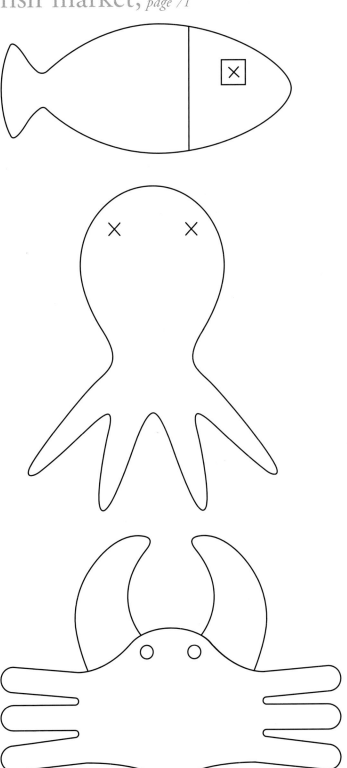

acknowledgments

Special thanks to Lyna Farkas for creating the surface decoration samples featured in the book's Basic Techniques section.

contributors

Thanks to the talented designers and artisans who helped develop the sewing, woodworking, and general do-it-yourself projects that appear throughout the book.

Now retired to his dream shop in the mountains of western North Carolina, **MIKE CALLIHAN** is a graduate mechanical engineer who earned his living in the plastic injection molding industry. His first love in woodworking is building all manner of furniture, ranging in style from Shaker to classic 18th-century reproductions. Though he has no formal training in furniture building, Mike grew up in the woodworking industry, working in his father's cabinet shop. In addition to furniture building, he enjoys woodcarving, turning, and cabinetmaking.

JEAN TOMASO MOORE is a part-time multimedia artist who has been creating art in one form or another for as long as she can remember. She lives with a humble and patient husband in the beautiful hills of Asheville, North Carolina.

TRACY MUNN is a sewing dynamo who stays constantly busy doing custom upholstery work in the barn she recently converted into a studio. After running her own dressmaking business in South Carolina for years, she moved to North Carolina in 1995. She now focuses on sewing dresses for her granddaughters, Chaley and Chloe, who live much too far away in Minnesota.

TERRY TAYLOR lives and works in Asheville, North Carolina, as an editor and project coordinator for Lark Books. He is a prolific designer and exhibiting artist and works in media ranging from metals and jewelry to paper crafts and mosaics.

index

Accents, 28–29

Borders. *See* Wallpapering

Carpets, 88–90, 91

Combing. *See* Surface decoration techniques

Decorative themes: animals, 16–29; astronomy, 30–39; color and patterns, 72–91; flowers, 40–59; maritime, 60–71; storage, creative, 91–109

Design considerations: child's age, 10–11; furniture to grow with, 14; safety, 15; size and scale, 12; use of color, 13

Fabric projects, 18–22, 23–25, 25, 34–35, 39, 41–44, 46, 48–50, 54–55, 66–67, 70–71, 74–75, 78–79, 80, 84–86, 92–95, 96–98, 104–105, 108–109

Floors, 62, 88–90

Flower pots, soft sculpture project, 41–44; painted readymade, 51

Furniture projects: bed pockets, 92–95; cabana cover, 66–67; caddies, rolling, 19–22; canopy, 39; chairs, 47, 52–53, 54–55; chalkboard, 87; crib organizer, 108–109; cupboard, 57; cupboard curtains, 80; desk, 102–103; drawers, 106–107; dresser, 76–77; toy box cover, 104–105

Lighting projects: lamp, 59; light cover, 74–75; light fixture, 36–38

Mirror, 58

Mobiles, 23–25, 25, 46

Painting basics: floors, 113; furniture, 114–115; walls, 110–112

Painting projects: 33, 51, 54–55, 56–67, 61, 62, 63, 64–65, 68–69, 76–77, 82–83, 87, 88–90, 91, 106–107

Paper mâché project, 58

Paper project, 59

Photo transfer projects: mobile, 46; chair, 47

Pickling, project using, 63

Rag rolling. *See* Surface decoration techniques

Rugs. *See* Carpets

Sand pails, 63

Shades, 34-35

Sleeping tent, 84–86

Sponging. *See* Surface decoration techniques

Sponging project, 33

Stamping. *See* Surface decoration techniques

Stamping projects, 81–83, 88–90

Stenciling. *See* Surface decoration techniques

Stencil projects, 27–32

Storage projects, 19–22, 34–35, 48–50, 56–57, 92–95, 96–98

Surface decoration techniques, 116–117

Tote, 96–98

Toys, push or pull, 28–29; cloth, 70–71

Quilt, stenciled, 27

Wall decoration projects, 18, 28–29, 48–50, 64–65

Wallpapering: basics, 118-119

Weathering, project using, 61

Window treatments: curtains, 78–80; shades, 35

Woodworking projects, 19–22; 28–29; 99